AVID

READER

PRESS

CHERISHED BELONGING

THE
HEALING
POWER OF
LOVE IN
DIVIDED
TIMES

GREGORY BOYLE

AVID READER PRESS

NEW YORK LONDON TORONTO SYDNEY NEW DELHI

Avid Reader Press
An Imprint of Simon & Schuster, LLC
1230 Avenue of the Americas
New York, NY 10020

First Avid Reader Press hardcover edition November 2024

AVID READER PRESS and colophon are trademarks of Simon & Schuster, LLC

Simon & Schuster: Celebrating 100 Years of Publishing in 2024

For information about special discounts for bulk purchases,
please contact Simon & Schuster Special Sales
at 1-866-506-1949 or business@simonandschuster.com.

The Simon & Schuster Speakers Bureau can bring authors to your live event.
For more information or to book an event contact the Simon & Schuster Speakers Bureau
at 1-866-248-3049 or visit our website at www.simonspeakers.com.

Interior design by Ruth Lee-Mui

Manufactured in the United States of America

1   3   5   7   9   10   8   6   4   2

Library of Congress Control Number: 2024944225

ISBN 978-1-6680-6185-5
ISBN 978-1-6680-6187-9 (ebook)

For

EILEEN *and* MICHAEL

MAUREEN *and* JEFF

STEVE *and* THERESA

ANNIE *and* JIM

MEG *and* PAT

KELLY *and* GRANT

PAUL *and* JOY

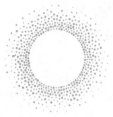

CONTENTS

INTRODUCTION

I HAD THE AISLE SEAT, EXIT ROW, WITH TWO HOMIES FLYING
home to Los Angeles from Philadelphia. As people boarded, I could
see a very tall man making his way down the aisle. I tried to read the
words printed on his shirt. "PHILLY IS EVERYBODY." I'm heart-
ened. I think kinship, connection, exquisite mutuality, and, yes, we
belong to each other. As he got closer, I could see that the T-shirt
ACTUALLY said, "PHILLY VS. EVERYBODY." Shoot. We were
so close there.

How do we arrive at a place and tenor of community that as-
serts: Nobody VS. Anybody? This is, in fact, a good definition of the
kinship of God. Normalization and polarization have both proven
corrosive to kinship. Musician Taj Mahal used to say: "Everybody is
somebody. Nobody is nobody." No Us and Them, just Us. This is,
indeed, God's dream come true.

The homies recently changed my Siri voice to that of an Irish woman. I'm taken back to my relatives in Dunloy, County Antrim, Northern Ireland, every time I hear her. I was preaching, not long ago, in a packed church prior to a fundraiser and awards event, and in the middle of my homily, during a pause in my preaching, comes this amplified, sweet Irish voice from my left pants pocket: "I do not understand what you're saying." I told my cell phone, "Join the club," and fumbled to power her off.

But this same voice guides me in all my GPS needs. I'm directed, for example, to "pull into the car park." She'll warn me on the freeway, "Accident up ahead," or "Road work," or "Hazard ahead," or some other potential obstacle in my journey. Then comes a pause, a brief beat, and I await, breathlessly, for instructions to navigate the obstacle. Then she says with a lilting voice, "You're still on the fastest route." This message never fails to console me, and I proceed apace.

I don't understand this to mean that I'm on the quickest route. I know that I am on the "surest" one. This path is certain to get me there.

I recently spoke on a panel at the *LA Times* Festival of Books with Rabbi Naomi Levy and my friend, *LA Times* columnist Steve Lopez. I told the crowd that two unwavering principles held at Homeboy Industries were the following: 1) Everyone is unshakably good (no exceptions) and 2) We belong to each other (no exceptions). Then I posited: "Now, do I think all our vexing and complex social dilemmas would disappear if we embraced these two notions?" I paused, then continued, "Yes, I do." And the entire audience exploded in laughter. I was startled. When the laughter subsided, I repeated quietly: "Yes. I do."

These two ideas allow us to roll up our sleeves so that we can actually make progress. So that we can love without measure and without regret. So that we can cultivate a new way of seeing. We finally understand that the answer to every question is, indeed, compassion. How else do we bridge the great polarizing divide that presents itself now, as a clear and present danger in our country? Poet Amanda Gorman writes, "Our only enemy is that which would make us enemies to each other." If all our efforts don't pull us together as allies, then folks will fill in the blanks and presume we are adversaries. Paramount for all of us, at the moment, is how to forge a way out of our intractable impasses. Obstacles and hazards abound. With a cherishing love, we're still on the fastest route.

I suppose I am writing this book because of that one question I always get at some point during the Q and A period after a talk I've given. My friend Pema Chödrön, Buddhist teacher and nun, also gets a version of the same question about what she calls "Mr. T." It's a question about the alarming divide and this excruciating impasse in which we find ourselves at the moment. I never feel like I adequately answer the issue for people. I often wondered how I would more fully answer this frequently asked question if I had more time. I want to take a stab here. Consequently, this book will be different from previous ones. This book hopes to see some horizon above the impasse. After all, an impasse is a situation in which no progress can be made. I'm writing now with a longing to dissolve the deadlock.

For many years now, in my talks, I refer to a saying by Mother Teresa: "Mother Teresa tells us that the problem in the world is that we've just forgotten that we belong to each other." I was speaking somewhere and, I threw that line out. A local newspaper did its research and, in the paper the next day, printed the full and accurate quote: "If we have no peace, it is because we have forgotten that we belong to each other." This simple principle seemed to unlock a door for much that ails our country and world.

If there are people living in tents on Main Street . . . it is because we have forgotten. If there are more and more fentanyl overdoses . . . suicides . . . hate crimes . . . homophobic assaults . . . election conspiracies . . . anti-Semitic rants . . . homicides . . . massacres in Israel and Palestine . . . it is because we have forgotten. If only we can land on a common story, it just might propel us to connection and belonging.

This book hopes to address the existential moment in which we find our country (and world). It seeks to remind ourselves of what we deeply want and how that longing connects us to each other on a route sure to lead us to our destination. It encourages a search for wholeness and a collective patience with each other as we all engage in healing and mend our severed belonging. It is not my intention in this book to "win some argument." Nigel, who did twenty-five years of a thirty-five-year sentence, speaks of the need for "vision casting." He calls it "languaging." I suppose one needs to make the case and put words together. How strong is any argument, if we're afraid to make it? Our quest for wholeness is not a destination that we arrive at; it's a journey we keep at.

For forty years, I have been accompanying gang members in Los Angeles. Near as anyone can tell, there are 1,100 gangs and 120,000 gang members in the county of Los Angeles. It feels like most of them have my cell phone number. Nearly ten thousand people a year walk through our doors at Homeboy Industries, wanting to explore a new life. I include in this number the many who come for a tour, to volunteer, and to support our efforts in the café and store. They, too, are exploring something new.

After thirty-six years in the city, Homeboy Industries has backed its way into now becoming the largest gang intervention, rehab, and reentry program on the planet. We never set out to do that. It just happened. Like Isaiah underscores: "While from behind, a voice shall sound in your ears: this is the way; walk in it." It was definitely a voice from behind, not some clarity in front of us.

Sometimes when I'm being introduced at a talk, the host will say all of the above but also add "the most successful." I never say this. I make certain that phrase is never inserted into our material. Successful? Who knows? I always want us to become less outcome obsessed and more faithful to loving. We are outcome aware but not outcome-driven. What drives us is the person in front of us. After all, Jesus never heals a crowd of people. Just one person at a time. Oddly, the very idolatry of outcomes can keep progress distant. We hope against hope that beyond professionalism is a person-centered approach. "Practice-based evidence" rather than "evidence-based outcomes." Outcomes don't define who we are. Same with organizations as with people. What if we didn't punish the wounded but, rather, sought to heal them? In American society, we are faced with broken people, and we have chosen to build prisons to accommodate them. What if we did the reverse? We want to commit to creating a culture and community of cherished belonging. I'm not suggesting that Homeboy is the answer, but we might have stumbled upon the question. As Daniel Berrigan says, "Know where to stand and stand there." Homeboy just wants to keep standing there.

Glancing back at these thirty-six years, I remember well the hostility directed at Homeboy in our first ten years. Our daily diet was replete with death threats, bomb threats, and hate mail. None of it, of course, from gang members, who always saw us as a sign of hope and an exit ramp. But to those who demonized this population, we were fraternizers with the enemy. It was always a short hop to demonize

Homeboy for walking with the demonized. Then everything changed overnight.

In October of 1999, our first social enterprise, Homeboy Bakery, burned to the ground. The next day, the *Los Angeles Times* declared that Homeboy Industries didn't belong to "Fr. Greg Boyle," but to the entire city of Los Angeles. In an instant, we went from reviled to watching Homeboy Industries get hoisted onto the shoulders of the city. This tipping point enabled us to build a new bakery and our headquarters, where we have set up for sixteen years now.

COVID-19 arrived for us all in 2020. For the poor, the pandemic wasn't an inconvenience, but the great exacerbator of despair, trauma, and mental illness. We also discovered that privacy was not a luxury afforded to those on the margins. We discovered that our vulnerability was not equal. This inequality fomented more violence and death in the inner cities. Homeboy tried to stand in this therapeutic place, honoring the beloved belonging to which we are all called. In the wake of the COVID crisis, cities were again tempted to crack down on crime as they have in the past, regardless of the ineffectiveness of that effort. Homeboy shines a light that reminds us that a civilized people cares for each other. We will care or we will 'cuff. As always, we will find gang violence in communities with historically high levels of concentrated disadvantage and disinvestment. We want to spotlight the need to raise the advantage and make investments and then watch what happens to rage, violence, and despair.

Homeboy represents a proof of concept. We have no interest in scaling up and becoming the McDonald's of gang intervention programs (with over five billion gang members served). Instead, we have spent the last sixteen years nurturing into existence the Global Homeboy Network: a loose band of partners who take Homeboy's model of a community of tenderness and apply it to local, vexing, and complex social issues like homelessness, disaffected youth, folks suffering from mental anguish or substance use disorder, returning citizens, etc. We have over three hundred "partners" in the United States and fifty outside the country. We convene as many folks as we can hold at our Global Homeboy Network Gathering, held for three days every summer. We explore together this *modo de proceder*, as Saint Ignatius would say. What would happen if we applied the culture of Homeboy to all that ails us as a society and as a world? It's not that we think Homeboy is (as the homies say) "all that and a bag of chips." We aren't. But as Dan McKanan said of the Catholic Worker Movement: "It's more of an organism than an organization." That also feels right about Homeboy.

Homeboy reflects elements that we think can put us on the fastest route of healing, good diagnoses, relational wholeness, and cherished belonging. When we embrace relational wholeness, our divisions tremble. We aspire to be on the lookout for the secret wholeness in each other. We zero in on the precious soulfulness in everyone. We see as God sees. Vice president of operations, homie Steve Avalos, says, "A structured place is a safe place. It is there that we see the homies' hearts until they can see their own . . . then they leave here, and they see other hearts." The homies don't need saving. They need healing. I am certain that I am not a healer. I'm equally certain that at Homeboy, healing happens.

Being a part of something positive rewires the brain. Fresh neural pathways get forged. From a healthy place, we all discover that separation is folly. I never call us an "agency." It feels too bureaucratic. Agency, tools, curriculum—all of this is secondary. It's what we do. But a community of cherished belonging is who we are. A homie,

Marcus, told a classroom filled with inner-city teenagers, "If love was a place, it would be Homeboy."

I recognize that the word "rehabilitation" is deficient as well. It implies restoring someone to some former privilege, a state of pre-damage. A previous moment where injury didn't exist. That time and moment basically wasn't there for our folks. Since 1988, I've buried 261 people who were killed because of gang violence. Most were buried in what I call the decade of death (1988–1998). Pádraig Ó Tuama says that in Northern Ireland, the Irish word that we translate into English as "troubles" really means "bereavements." I understand this distinction.

In the early days, I'd walk my very poor parish, comprising two extremely large and densely populated public housing developments. Then, in later years, on my black beach cruiser bike, I would "patrol" my parish and the eight warring gangs there. I've recounted many stories from those days in previous books. Today, gang members who came up through the Homeboy program now run the place, and I meander as an "emeritus something or other." From founder to flounder. We are healthier at Homeboy whenever we move from power-hoarding to power-sharing. It's worth getting used to. "We are a power-building organization," Steve Avalos says. "There is a process, but there is also a practice."

One of our homie vice presidents, José Arellano, puts it this way: "This is beautiful work, but it's not always pretty." True dat. Recently, I received a generic letter from prison, from an inmate wanting more information and a support letter for his parole board. We get thousands of these requests a year. He writes in the letter that he has "read the Homeboy book" (presumably *Tattoos On The Heart*) and then "Please send mines to Fr. Greg. To my understanding, he's the program's Art Laboe."

I give talks to audiences around the world. My Jesuit community has become Southwest Airlines. An old friend texted me about a conversation she had with a woman who asked, "What does Father Greg's wife think of all his traveling?" I wrote back: "Tell her she's glad that my ass is out of the house." On these trips, more often than not I bring along two homies or homegirls or couples to share what happens at Homeboy. Consequently, many of the stories here are culled from "travels with homies." Before a talk in Pasadena, a man came up to me and said, "Homeboy Industries has gentled the culture of Los Angeles." The brave men and women who choose to walk through our doors are responsible for such a thing.

Planes are odd communities. You can't help but have your annoyance gland constantly activated. The cluelessness, the invasion of personal space. The nervous flyer who can't stop talking. Really. The woman who keeps pushing her call button thinking the flight attendant is her waitress or personal valet. The guy who keeps jumping up to reach into the overhead compartment. Of course, the passenger in the window seat needs to go to the restroom nine times; she won't stop drinking iced teas. You're going to eat that on this plane? Seriously?

So I ask myself: Is everybody on this plane good? Yes, unshakably. Anyone wicked or evil? Nope. Is there anyone on board who does not belong to us. No.

So we can begin.

Above all, this book explores the question: Why have we made so little progress? And, yes, I agree with Barack Obama, who said at the end of his two terms, "If you think we haven't made progress, then you're not paying attention." Maybe it's more precise to ask: What keeps us, consistently, from making progress? This book posits that some very specific sets of thinking impede us. When we've made progress, it's because we've named things correctly and then pointed the way.

We don't make progress when we demonize. We should abandon that altogether, and in all circumstances refuse to do it. A mother and stepfather tortured and killed their young son. A candidate for district attorney said, "They are bad people. And I use the word 'people' lightly. They are nothing short of monsters." Surely, we can hold something as horrible and still not make monsters of anyone. Demonizing keeps us from solutions. Plus, it's always the opposite of how God sees.

We should likewise jettison the idea that there could be such a thing as good people and bad people. And finally, we must include every single person in our circle of belonging. This isn't a book that merely advances Rodney King's "Can we all get along?" notion. It wants to underscore that when we demonize and divide the world into "good and bad people" and exclude folks from cherished belonging, progress gets stopped in its tracks. These notions end all conversation. But with the clear goal of a community of cherished belonging, dialogue gets jump-started. There is nothing in our path to shut it down.

At Homeboy Industries, we're always trying to pry the criminal justice system away from violence and punishment, overpolicing and mass incarceration, and bend it toward healing, repair, and restoration. Heal wounds rather than punish them. Our tendency, to date, as a society, is to medicalize and criminalize unlivable lives. We've nearly outlawed the hopeless. This punishment system needs to be dismantled.

We are all seeking a more powerful narrative of belonging. Our next frontier at Homeboy Industries is to imagine Hope Village. We want to create a neighborhood of services that can truly stand as an alternative to incarceration. Beyond just a campus expansion, this renewed narrative of cherished belonging might serve as a model for the country beyond the punitive and instead represent a heightened reverence for the complex causes of crime. Instead of bars and cells, we lay out a welcoming community that tries to soothe mental anguish, substance use disorder, and an underlying despair. Rather than the tribalism that excludes and punishes, the new narrative proposes a village that cherishes.

Writing is arduous, at least for me. It is very difficult to find time to dedicate to this task, and often, when I read what I have drafted thus far, my stuff feels like it's been written by a committee and I wasn't invited to the meetings. Annie Dillard says that writing is like sitting up with a sick friend. I've spent many a night with my ailing pal. I suppose I wrote these pages in response to those endless questions, after my talks, about the division in our country and the polarizing malaise that has us stupefied. But also, my writing kept trying to find "the straight line."

On September 13, 2023, Danelo Cavalcante was captured. He was a Brazilian national, convicted of murder, who had escaped from Chester County Prison not far from Philadelphia. He evaded capture for two weeks. On the day he was apprehended, the sheriff declared: "Our nightmare is finally over, and the good guys won." This book wants to assert that one can draw a straight line from that sheriff's statement—"the good guys won"—to the very lack of progress we fail to make in crime, mass incarceration, homelessness, fentanyl overdoses, gangs, mental illness, the political divide, etc.

I suppose seventy is the new fifty, but still. Geezerdom has set in and I'm feeling mortality skulking around my house. My dad died at seventy. Like many folks my age, I've had random bouts with cancer and remission. Some days, you just feel old. A homie stage-whispered to another, in my hearing, "G is so old, he's still on AOL." Another said, when I celebrated fifty years a Jesuit, "Damn, that's a lot of reading." (I don't even know what that means.) A very weathered, tattooed homegirl, before she can introduce herself, breaks into tears: "You baptized me in Juvenile Hall"—trying to compose herself—"and now . . . I'm a grandma." Yes. That's a lot of reading.

I don't think I'm at death's door, but I find myself assessing things I believe as I inch toward that door. I believe the following things:

1. God is in the loving.
2. God IS inclusion.
3. Demonizing is always untruth.
4. We belong to each other.
5. Separation is an illusion.
6. Tenderness is the highest form of spiritual maturity.
7. "Kindness is the only non-delusional response to everything" (George Saunders).
8. Love your neighbor as you love your child.
9. We are all unshakably good.
10. A community of cherished belonging is God's dream come true.

For what it's worth, this book just wants to lure us to embracing God's heart and *punto de vista*. It proposes a mystical view that perhaps can lift us above those things that keep us apart. Nobody VS. Anybody. God's dream come true.

THE WILD ONE

I ASK SCRAPPY HOW HIS DAY WENT. HE PONDERS THE QUESTION before answering, "Today . . . I let God hold me by the hand."

I'd been told by our people that I need to be at KTLA VERY early. They are going to promote our 5K Walk/Run the following week and need me in the studio for the five-minute spot. Our press liaison, Nadia, has instructed Louie to join me and, I suppose, capture it all. He's our homie house photographer and somewhat famous for asking you to hold that pose for the time it takes cobwebs to form. I often snore loudly when he does this. It never seems to speed him up.

Louie is good company. "He be poppin' out with stuff," the homies say of him. He's unpredictable and can often take you on an unexpected *viaje*. I pick him up in front of the Homegirl Café. It's still dark. When we're on the freeway and well on our way, his phone rings. "It's Nadia," he tells me. "I better take it." Instantly, he affects the tone of someone barely rousing himself from very deep, REM sleep. "Ye . . . ah?" as drowsily as he can muster. Then he snaps to: "That's TODAY? . . . Damn . . . I just woke up." Nadia is quite possibly screaming. He suddenly perks up. "Just kidding. I'm driving with G now." Then he reassures her further. "Don't mind me. I'm in my terrible twos."

It's nice to catch up with him on our trek to the studio. I ask him about the state of things with his "baby mama" with whom he shares a son; their relationship has been contentious in the past. "I've decided to be strategic with her," he says. He doesn't want to fight with her. "I don't want to be bashful with her," which, as near as I can tell, means he doesn't want to verbally "bash her."

Louie takes all these shots of me—sitting in the greenroom, walking into the studio, shaking hands with the "talent." When I can, I feign nodding off as he tries to get the perfect shot.

On our way back to Homeboy, I swing by my childhood home to show Louie where all eight of us grew up. On the hundredth anniversary of the house, the extremely nice new owners invited my mom and all of us over for a huge party. When my mom, in her nineties, pulled up to the house in her wheelchair, she could see the owner had hung a small wooden sign on the portico with two tight chains that read: "The Boyle Home." My mother wept, and it took her a while to compose herself enough to come inside.

Louie sees the sign, still in place, thinks it's cool, leaps out of the car, gets the perfect (and lugubrious) shot, and then hops back in the car. "Let's get out of here, before they call the hounds."

The singular Meister Eckhart, mystic and priest (along with Saint Ignatius of Loyola, of course) is something of a recent spiritual father for me. He wanted to wake folks up and would often, in his preaching, say something ridiculous and outrageous as sort of an alarm clock. The Church at the time put him in the penalty box because he proposed a notion of God quite at odds with the Church's thinking. He was condemned a week after he died. The Church tried to maintain an image of the distant and aloof "Unapproachable God," and Eckhart insisted that the God we actually have was saying to us, clearly, "Approach. Come closer. Let me take you by the hand." Like Louie, who waits an eternity to bring us into focus, this God just wants to approach us, remind us of our goodness, and access us. The perfect shot.

Eckhart speaks of the "Wild One," the God ceaselessly surprising, whose care and delight in us is hugely outsized. The Church in his day (and perhaps currently) wanted to tame this wild God because the puny and distant version served their purpose. This God, like Louie, wants to take us on an unexpected *viaje*. By the hand. This God "be poppin' out with stuff." A domesticated, unapproachable God, however, will put your butt in a pew every Sunday. This wild, astonishing God may have more spacious plans for us.

We align the compass of our hearts with the energy of this wild God. We find the God of intimate welcome, generous hospitality. This God does not want to "bash" us. We are beckoned to see the intimacy of the unseen, and it allows us to live in the immediacy of wonder. It can delight in the terrible twos, no matter how old we are. The light inside of everything.

I go to anoint Esperanza on her deathbed. Pancreatic cancer brought her to this moment surrounded by family and friends. It was clear, before long, that her next breath would soon belong to God. It took me a minute to work through the crowd to apply the holy oil to her forehead and then to invite the gathered to all do the same.

Esperanza was my pal. Our point of connection were her two sons, Sammy and Luis, who were both gang members. I knew them from back in the day, when I had more hair, and when they were both causes of my rapid loss of it.

After the anointing, Luis and Sammy insist on walking me to my car. They're doing well now. Employed and with kids of their own, they seem to have found the path that leads to flourishing. We lean against my car, and the two brothers get teary as they retrieve memories of this stalwart woman. Sammy, the younger and wilder of the two, recalls a moment. He's sitting across from his mom in the visitors' room at Central Juvenile Hall. He's fifteen years old. The two of them are sitting at the lonely end of a long table and she cannot take her eyes off her kid. It is all gaze and little conversation. At one point she asks, in Spanish, if the guard is looking their way. Sammy tells her no. In an instant, she reaches into her bra and deftly removes a small, still-warm burrito from Al & Bea's, a Boyle Heights institution. ("It's the special ones," Sammy clarifies, "the chile relleno ones.") Just as deftly, Sammy grabs the burrito and pulls it down under the table. Furtively, when the guard is distracted, he'll take a bite while his mom smiles placidly. Love is a radiant light. It is the light inside of everything.

Eckhart thought that human beings had this ability to think in the divine mind. Esperanza engaged in this intimate participation with God. The divine presence is awakened in her. This "Voluptuous God" is let loose and liberated from our tired notions. Now we are able to connect to the passionate longing of God. The will of God, if you will. We can give marching orders to the God that keeps us from inclusion and loving acceptance. Sammy was not just fed that morning at Juvenile Hall; he was given access to something. He was captured by the belonging of God, as surely and slowly as Louie brings his subject into focus. God's pleasure in us is altogether reliable, what John O'Donohue calls coming home to your soul, to the house that you never left. He emphasizes that this is not a "spiritual journey . . . it's a rhythm." O'Donohue urges, "Enter the quiet immensity of your own presence." Sammy in this tender moment is more than fed—he's in rhythm with himself and fortified. He's untouchable.

Part of the quest is to be freed from everything that is not God. Eckhart thought we should rid ourselves of the irrelevant stuff, the tired views of God and religious language that block the pores of our soul. Richard Rohr says that your image of God creates you. Our God is self-effacing. We aren't. This may be one of the reasons why we have such a hard time connecting to the God of love. God is not needy. We are. God does not long to be liked. We do. God is never fishing for a compliment. That's our thing. Homies are endlessly insisting, for example, that everything happens for a reason. God is behind every reasonableness and everything unreasonable. When the opportunity affords itself, I will tell homies that God is too busy loving them to have any time left for orchestration. Sometimes we are saddled with an image of God that does not create us in God's image.

I'm sitting near an older woman at a Fantastic Sams waiting for a haircut. She takes a call from her son. She speaks only Spanish, and every time her son presents, I suppose, some calamity or misfortune that has befallen him, she keeps saying, "*Dios manda*": God is in charge, or also, perhaps, God is sending this. It can mean both. I suspect we sometimes insist that "God is my co-pilot" so we don't have to fly the plane. "*Aquí mando yo*" (I call the shots here) is what the stern father or strict husband says tirelessly. Clearly, we need to sidestep what Mirabai Starr calls the "Abusive Father God" and, indeed, replace it with the ceaselessly delighting and sustaining One. The prophet Hosea would say that God wounds us, then heals us. God strikes us, Hosea maintains, then binds our wounds. When God is the cause of everything, it allows for the abusive father who beats our ass, then wipes our tears. A reset is in order. For even when we find ourselves less than delightful, God does not delight in us less.

In a recent *New York Times Magazine* interview, eighty-seven-year-old primatologist Jane Goodall said, "Traditional faith will have you believe in a loving God, and when I look at what's happening on the planet, I think if there is a God like that, is he playing with us?" Not sure "traditional faith" actually wants us to believe that, but a reset can refine our thinking here.

I realize now, after all, that I DO believe in an all-powerful God. I always thought one had to choose between an all-loving God or an all-powerful one. But this power does not reside in God's rescue of us nor in God's choosing to change outcomes; rather, God's power is found in the sustaining love that is always extended our way and accompanies us. Not a God who intervenes but one who energizes us to act. Go ahead, fly the plane. We can feel God leaning into our very own well-being and longing for it to flourish. The all-loving God IS powerful. We don't have to choose. The power is in the loving.

It is necessary, however, to release our hold on the categorical. We don't really know the God of love like we might know algebra or how to cook spaghetti carbonara or how to balance our checkbook. Knowing the God of love is a different kind of knowing. We locate access to this knowledge when we let God take our hand. We're invited to participate and let ourselves go down the slide into the pool. God hopes we'll grab that hand on the way down. The meaning of the word "Islam" is "surrender." We go down the slide surrendering our entire being to this Wild One. We no longer settle for the partial God but hold out for the Spacious One. Then we find our authentic core, in undeniably resembling this expansive God. And what could be more wild, and surprising?

I asked homie Fabian how he prays. He tells me, "Sometimes I just sit there and say, 'Hold me.'" In this stillness, Fabian rests and then abides. The quiet immensity. Pascal said that most of our troubles occur from our inability to sit still in a room. I suspect it's how we "let" God hold our hand. The stillness gives us access to the God of love. Nothing in the universe, Eckhart tells us, resembles God so much as silence. Like any parent who is helpless in a mountain of circumstances, God's promise remains: I will carry you. I will hold you. God creates us as the Beloved, and in this we find a roomy capacity to love. We become habitually established in God's tenderness. Hidden with Christ in God. To be held is to be habitually established in love. God is a God who loves through all loves. In fact, God will reach into her bra and provide a warm burrito—you know, the special kind. This very sustenance binds us in the freedom of love and has power enough. Thomas Merton was gentle with people because God was gentle with him. We receive this sustenance also, so that we can sustain each other.

We still have to sometimes plod our way through Scripture passages in the daily liturgy that are often at odds with our deep, soulful sense of the God of love. We suffer through, say, parts of Tobit that suggest that God is as judgmental as I am. (Spoiler alert: God isn't.) We hear that God is "slow to anger." But we know God . . . is NO to anger. The God we have does not need anger management. I saw this *New Yorker* cartoon where several inhabitants of heaven are standing on clouds surrounding God in the middle, who seems to be laughing.

One of these souls says to another, "I don't fear the wrath of God, but his nervous laugh scares the hell out of me." But the truth of the matter is this: the infinite love of God is always trying to access us. Mystic Mechtild of Magdeburg suggests that the God of love is powerless to do otherwise. God chooses this powerlessness. God will be uninterrupted in loving. Unstoppable. There is no nervous laugh.

We unlearn what we need to unlearn. So, Noah builds the ark because God looked at "the wickedness of humanity" and said, "Oh boy . . . do I ever regret having created these people." We know that our Wild God never felt or said any such thing. Wisdom clarifies: "For you love all things that are, and loathe nothing you have made . . . Your imperishable spirit is in all things." The light inside of everything. The God of love doesn't have a range of responses: "Oh, I like that." "I don't like that at all." Rather, this Wild God of ours has a singularity of response to us. The Tender One says so clearly: I will carry you and sustain you in love, no matter what. You are irreplaceable, unrepeatable, and of unlimited worth. Augustine puts it this way: "You love us like there is only one of us."

At a house where I was leading a weekend retreat, the first reading was the story of Abraham and Isaac. It begins, "God put Abraham to the test." I opened my homily by telling the congregation that life provides us with endless "tests," but not once has the God of love ever thrown one our way. Not ever. "And besides," I told them, "any father who hears God tell him to kill his son is mentally ill." They applauded, which surprised me. I proceeded, then, to preach on the Transfiguration.

Deuteronomy says God "tests us with affliction." Once we have a palpable, heartfelt experience of the God of love, we know that can't be true. The Israelites are told that God "let you be afflicted by hunger." Nope. Shit and hunger happen, but mainly because we don't share of our abundance nor keep a watchful eye on each other's well-being. God has no interest in pulling the rug out from underneath us.

In a big city cathedral, I drop by for Sunday mass. The priest is preaching on Matthew 10, where the disciples are being sent out. Then he ends the homily with this: "In the last part of this Gospel passage, Jesus utters the scariest words you have ever heard. But we can't pick and choose. Jesus says this: 'If you acknowledge me, then I will acknowledge you before the Heavenly Father . . . but if you DENY me, I will deny you before the Heavenly father.' Think about that!" And he ends the homily. Of course, you pick and choose. We are supposed to. It's what the homie Sergio, my spiritual director, calls "the mystical filter." Jesus used it when he quoted the Hebrew Bible. He repeated the lines that gave him life and left behind the stuff that didn't. Like a wrathful God. No one who knows the God of love thinks that "denying" us is even in God's lexicon. No parent, after all, would ever deny her kid, and how much less so would God? In seventy years of living, I can't call up a single moment in John or the Synoptics where Jesus said something that scared me. Again, Mechthild says that "God wants to rest weightlessly in our soul." A lightness of being, not weighing us down with fearful foreboding.

In Islam, Allah has ninety-nine names. Monikers like "the Compassionate," "the Opener of the Heart," and "the Merciful." Names you won't find among the ninety-nine are "the Wrathful One," "the Punisher," or "the Eternally Disappointed One." Much less "the Chomping at the Bit to Deny You One." In Jewish mysticism, God's very nature is infinite compassion, and it is this merciful face of God that is imprinted on the human heart. God is compassionate and merciful, always and in everything.

For the past many years, some thirty members of my Class of '72 at Loyola High School gather for a weekend retreat. Bob Barry, who sat a couple desks ahead of me in school ("Barry, Bennett, Boyle"), started the tradition. When he died too young from a brain tumor, we named the gathering The Bob Barry Invitational Retreat. I guide the reflections, and there's a lot of sharing. We're all geezers now, and a handful of these guys have buried their wives. Others have been married for forty to forty-five years. At one point in the sharing, a classmate says, "I need to listen to my wife more."

Another man seconds him: "I need to listen to MY wife more."

Then Shawn Bennett (Barry, Bennett, Boyle) says, "All this talk of listening to your wives reminds me of a story. A man is driving up a winding mountain road. A woman is driving down the road. When she passes the man, she yells out the window, 'PIG.' And the man yells back, 'BITCH.' Then the man makes a hairpin turn, and there in the middle of the road is a huge pig. He crashes into the pig, has a huge accident, and dies." Shawn concludes, "The moral of the story is . . . listen to women more."

It's good advice. I've taken it. I've immersed myself lately in women mystics, such as Teresa of Ávila, Dame Julian of Norwich, and Mechthild of Magdeburg, to name just three. "Love begets love," Teresa writes. Mystics found an anchor within, born of a love that can't be agitated. These women found a Christ consciousness and oneness in their rendezvous with the God of love. It drew them to see differently. They saw the world as God's body. It becomes an all-embracing cherishing that turns outward to the world, what Spinoza calls "a disposition for benevolence." With any luck, we sidestep our egos and allow all mystical moments to move outside ourselves. These women mystics knew that self-absorption drained their life and vitality. Mechtild envisioned instead the soul losing itself in love. Teresa felt the soul was our deepest identity. We should safeguard ourselves from being exiled from our souls. These women welcomed the tenderness of God, then vigorously poured that out in love. Teresa brings *Interior Castle* to this conclusion: "When one reaches the highest degree of human maturity, one has only one question left: How can I be helpful?" Like the bodhisattva vow, you choose to put others first and just be helpful. Outward. Onward.

One of the many magnets that adorn our refrigerator in my Jesuit community is one of Jesus preaching the Sermon on the Mount. In this pious, 1950s illustration of Jesus addressing the throngs on the hillside, Jesus says: "Okay, everyone. Now listen carefully. I don't want to end up with four different versions of this." Different versions frighten us. We think they will take us down some *Rashomon* rabbit hole, and somehow we won't know the truth. We won't know what really happened. The "mystical filter" helps us leave behind reading scripture literally and instead start to take scripture seriously. What gets revealed is indeed luminous and spacious and a glimpse of the expansive heart of the God of love. Of course we "pick and choose" because human beings are involved. Otherwise, we handle poisonous snakes blithely or we continue to prevent women from full inclusion in the Church.

The mystical lens helps us sort through the Bible, putting aside the stuff we just don't buy. I call it "finding the invitation." It's in there somewhere. Otherwise, we get tripped up by a wrathful God or distracted by Jesus thinking the guy with epilepsy is possessed by a demon. Or maybe we just can't get past the King, who magnanimously invites folks from the highways and byways to the feast, only for the man, who is apparently wearing shorts, a Hawaiian shirt, and flip-flops, to be taken outside and beaten. Find the invitation. What are we being invited to? Well, it's a banquet. Leave it at that. Use your mystical lens. God doesn't indict. God invites. Like the tired joke Ronald Reagan always told about the pile of horse manure. The kid says, "There has to be a pony in here somewhere." We use the mystical filter and find the invitation. It's in there somewhere.

What we get most wrong about God is that God can be pleased or displeased. I was directing a group retreat on Zoom during the pandemic, and one of the retreatants asked, "Well, isn't God pleased with some things and displeased with other things?"

I said: "We smile and frown, 'cuz we're human beings. God doesn't smile at us . . . God adores us. And God doesn't frown, either, 'cuz God's too busy adoring us." God's whole being says, "There is nothing you can do to make me stop loving you." We want to be rooted in this loving presence. Find the pony. Feel God's adoration. Julian of Norwich called it "Oneing." Gregory of Nyssa described it as "intimacy with God," where we are granted a taste of our oneness with God, and when we don't feel it, the taste only serves to galvanize our longing for more. Kabir said, "When the Guest is being searched for, it is the intensity of the longing for the Guest that does all the work." We are invited to love what God loves, which is quite different from doing things that please God. The prayer of our life is to lean toward the God of love and say, "Give me your eyes. Then all we'll see is glorious."

In our early morning email sessions every day, a reading from the day's liturgy triggered an immediate response from Sergio. "All this talk about forgiveness. I don't know. There's too much back and forth, back and forth, back and forth. I just want forth. Forth is mercy." Indeed, God is mercy. Or, as Merton says, "Mercy within mercy within mercy." Forgiveness is mercy in a minor key. Mercy is love without expectations. Mercy is all "forth" with no concern for return.

At Homeboy, we try to invite folks to the mystical mind, then we find God, less and less "out there" and more and more "in close" as Meister Eckhart suggests. It is challenging to find this God. I type "God" in a text and it autocorrects "GIF." But the God who wants to be found is the God of love. We find the ground of oneness there. Which is less about HOW God is and more about WHERE God is: in the loving. We align the compass of our hearts there.

The Trumper insurrectionist, after testifying at a January 6 congressional hearing, posts a photograph of him shaking the hand of one of the injured cops and apologizing to him. He shares the pic with the caption underneath: "Apology given . . . apology accepted." The cop reposts it with only the words: "Apology given."

There is no waiting in mercy, as there is in forgiveness. Apologies offered (after waiting). Apologies accepted (after waiting). Forgiveness is the raft, but mercy is the shore. We want to get to the shore. Mercy is letting go. Forgiveness is holding on. God never waits for us to get things right before loving us. It is the father running to his kid on the road and he's already planning in his head the seating arrangements at the fatted calf dinner. God doesn't wait for us to do something or to stop doing something. The God we have does not play hard to get. All love . . . no waiting. Just "forth." Why settle for forgiveness, when we can hold out for mercy?

I heard a preacher in Lakeside Chautauqua speak of "the grace of the wooing God who welcomes and includes everybody and brings us all together in Christ." God is infinitely in love with us and wants only to make that connection. A Trappist nun, before she died, prayed: "My God—help me accept how you see me—no matter how beautiful it is." As my friend Chris Hoch says, "The homies are used to a 'Department of Corrections' God. We want to propose a 'Department of Connections' God." We are being "wooed" to see this.

The very humble generosity of God deflects and says, gently, "Why are you looking at me?" God's loving expansiveness wants us to look at each other. To be the very generosity of God and to nurture each other into becoming a community of cherished belonging. We receive the sustenance, then choose to sustain each other. Catherine of Siena heard Christ tell her, "On two feet you must walk my way; on two wings you must fly to heaven." She interpreted this to mean: love God and neighbor. This is the ultimate victory of God's love over division, suffering, and death. Moreover, we come to see that God only wants our happiness and not Her own. So, it's preposterous to think that "pleasing God" is even a thing, any more than displeasing is. No healthy parent thinks, *I exist so that my kids will please me.*

"Remember that time, Cara, when Beaver threw that big-ass rock through my windshield?" The *vato* skipping down memory lane is Wicho. He, Cara, Shorty, and I are having dinner. These two homies haven't seen Cara in twenty-five years. When these guys first met her as teenagers, she was an earnest twenty-four-year-old from Boston. Then she was my "number two" at Homeboy for ten years. We are recalling snapshots from the last quarter of a century.

"Whoa, wait a minute!" Cara applies the brakes to Wicho's account. "You're jumping into the very middle of the story."

At the time, they were in our storefront office on First Street, and I was in Chicago giving a talk. "Norma was finishing a letter for Beaver for his PO," Cara tells us, "and he was waiting for it in that reception area in the front, with the crappy couch." In walks Wicho, full of his entire self. Wicho pivots, sees Beaver, and Beaver says, "You don't want to say anything now, do you?" Apparently, Wicho had "hit him up" earlier in the day, when Beaver was with his lady and baby.

At this point in the storytelling, Wicho smiles and pretends to hold up one of those neuralyzers from *Men in Black* and tries to freeze Cara and her memory bank. He keeps snapping it in her general direction as we all howl. "So, you race out of the office and go to your car and reach under the seat," Cara continues, saying that Beaver and half the staff flee to the back of the place and lock themselves in the job developer's office. Wicho rushes into the office brandishing something in his hand, covered in a towel. Wicho punctuates Cara's story again with an appearance of the neuralyzer.

Cara gets to the part when a homie in a wheelchair, stunned and imbalanced by the scene, falls out of his chair. "*La neta*, I felt bad when I saw him," Wicho contributes to Cara's account. "I dropped the rag and showed everybody it wasn't a gun, it was a club" (to lock the steering wheel). Beaver chases Wicho out of the office, then proceeds to take a huge clump of loose sidewalk and smash it through Wicho's front windshield. Now it's on. Wicho and Beaver commence to whale on each other, pummeling with all their force, until Cara manages to pull Beaver away. This petite blonde has her arms tightly squeezing Beaver from behind, while Wicho retrieves a wrench from the car. Now Cara dances Beaver around like a dervish, trying to avoid Wicho's wrench whacks.

The police come just in time to be too late. ("We were in the middle of a shift change.") Beaver and Wicho were long gone. When I got back from Chicago and heard about the incident, I tracked down Wicho, kicking it in his barrio late at night, and summoned him to my car. "G was mad as hell," he recounts at dinner.

Then Cara adds, "Yeah, and you came to me the next day and

said, 'I apologized to G.' And I said, 'TO G!? HE WASN'T EVEN THERE!'" We all laugh.

"*Spensa*, Cara," Wicho tells her, descending into the sheepish and smiling. In spite of everything, we can discover ourselves to be the capacity for God. Beyond discord and strife, we can find the light inside of everything, and we can inhabit that light. Mercy within mercy within mercy.

Jesus says plainly, "My joy yours. Your joy complete." This is all God wants for us. Being connected to this God of love is to know flourishing joy and fearlessness. We become God-intoxicated and recognize the holy in everything. We see as God thinks and love as God does. Black Elk tells us: "I saw more than I can tell and I understand more than I saw." This love is never imposed. It's always being offered. This infinite love of God is like being hit in the face with a sudden burst of sun, drawing us out of some darkened place or providing warmth when we're freezing. "To those in darkness," Isaiah says, "show yourselves."

A former student, who died too young and struggled too mightily, always referred to God as "M'Lady." Joy complete. M'Lady invites us to decide not to wait until we're dead to experience this union with God. It is precisely now that God calls us to a joyful urgency in love. An old Jesuit I knew would sign off with "Keep the faith and the joy that goes with it."

We don't so much rejoice as we live in joy always. We see as God sees and recognize that we are joy itself.

The Beloved is found everywhere and anywhere. This Beloved, in whom "we live and move and have our being," dwells in all that gets thrown at us every day. No need to pull out the neuralyzer. Savor it and remember it all. Everything is fertile enough to produce joy. This

Beloved is grounded in the tenderness of the Incarnation, a fecundity that is limitless. "M'Lady" reminds us always of the faithful kindness to which we are called and asks us to remember our blessed interconnectedness. From that sense of the Beloved, our kindness indeed increases the love in the world.

I suppose that because we have always insisted on a personified Deity, it naturally gets us into trouble. This is where our endless projections pop up. This God is soaked through with all our stuff: judgmental, pissed off, suspicious, disappointed. Long is the list of the traits we project. Yet we are infinitely being inched toward a melting into the heart of the Divine that finds only the merciful and holy in everything. We find what John of the Cross calls our "love longing." The God of love is peeking behind the curtain of every holy moment, and we just hope to be alert to it. This is our practice. The Divine fully alive in my kid, in that sunset, in the unexpected kindness. The God we experience is uncaged and freed of the personified Deity. We stand hopeful for a language large enough to carry us into a new territory of mystical seeing.

For two Octobers in a row, over fifty years ago, I picked grapes in Los Gatos, California. I was a Jesuit novice, and this was part of our formation. It was hard work, as we deftly took our grape knives, sliced a clump of purpleness into our aluminum bins, which were quite heavy when full, and dumped the contents into huge bins on a truck. At the end of the day, our jeans were drenched in grape juice and caked in mud and could almost literally stand by themselves in the basement of the old Novitiate building.

When it rained heavily, we didn't pick grapes. That second year of grape season, it was torrential for days on end. As the rain continued through the week, we were summoned one evening by Father Henri

Charvet, the old French Jesuit in charge of the grape harvest. He was visibly shaken and more severe than usual. "You must stop praying for rain!!" He was well-intentioned and a man of his time. Muffled titters roamed the room, for even as unseasoned as we were in the spiritual ways, we knew that the battle of the prayers (us for rain, Father Charvet for sun) was quite a ludicrous notion. How odd is the idea that we could sway our meteorologist God or that we even had such a God?

We pray to God: "Make this pain go away." We beseech: "I'm unemployed—make my unemployment go away." Our therapists utilize EMDR—eye movement desensitization and reprocessing therapy. It helps the homie retrieve a painful memory and seeks to change the way this memory is stored in the brain. A trainee, Joe, told me about it. Combined with eye movements and instructions from the therapist, he calls to mind a horrific memory. He notes that the pain is carried in his neck and chest. He thinks this whole thing is quite ridiculous, but he's nonetheless cooperative. The EMDR experience seems unremarkable to him. But the next morning, when Joe recalls the memory, there is no pain in his neck and chest. The memory is intact, but not the accompanying anguish. God does not make things go away. God helps us find our way through things. The homie Garry says, "Sometimes, we gotta go through it, to get to it."

To understand the God of love, we land on our own practice that helps us recalibrate our consciousness, to breathe in the infinite, creative presence of God. My friend Jim Finley calls it "God's presencing God's self." We try and align our whole being to this wild, ever-present God. This God doesn't play a causal role in anything, rain or shine, because God doesn't need to. God is not coercive. God is persuasive. God only invites and never indicts. Ricardo, charged with a very serious crime, was always struck that when his mom visited, she never asked, "Did you do it?" but rather, "Are you okay, son?" Not "Almighty God" but an all-loving God who constantly, in God's adoration of us, invites us to flourishing joy in community. THAT is almighty. This God has no interest in demanding that we do anything. God knows where the joy is and points us there. John O'Donohue says "God is beauty" and the root of the word "beauty" is "calling." God invites. So we try to listen to the invitation and follow the prompts of God, who is the compassion that understands. God says to us constantly: I won't be God without you.

Tonio was the youngest of nine children and the only gang member in the bunch. His father was old when he started to have kids and very old by the time Tonio landed in San Fernando Juvenile Hall. "He visited me every single Sunday I was in there. And I was there a gang of months. He never missed a visit." Tonio catches himself as he recalls, choking up. "He came one Sunday, like always. This time, some guys had beat me down and my eyes were nearly closed . . . mean-ass black, swollen eyes." He spoke of how his dad sees him and just begins to sob. When the weeping subsides, he looks at his boy, grabs his son's hands from across the table in the visiting room, and makes a declaration: "I'm never gonna give up on you." Tonio retrieves this image when asked to come up with a moment in his life that rhymed with God. Isaiah writes, "Enlarge the space for your tent . . . My love shall never leave you."

All of authentic spirituality is a homecoming. Home is the place where abandonment can't ever happen. Tonio's dad brought "home" to his incarcerated kid. We don't just walk each other home to wholeness; we are home to each other. My friend Adam Drake in Australia says when he visits youth in detention facilities, "they fully expect you to abandon them early. So their whole body language says: 'Get it

over with.'" Indeed, prisons have become a form of organized aban-
donment. Like my mom weeping at the little sign hanging from the
portico, we seek to return to a place of confident innocence, lush
beauty, and cherished belonging. It IS the home we never really left.
It becomes the place of gentle inwardness where we can hear the
words "I'm never gonna give up on you."

A homie wanted to know, "What's up with that Christmas carol:
'Come let us adore Him'? I mean . . . My God adores me." I'm okay
with changing the lyrics. "Come let us . . . allow God to adore us." To
let God hold us by the hand. This is a spacious and expansive God,
who is self-effacing enough to do the adoring. We find ourselves
nearly unraveled by such a God. God feels no threat in this role re-
versal.

One of the names the Zulus have for God gets translated as "Big
Big." That's right. We all believe in a God of second chances—though,
frankly, we give very few of them. We all believe in a God of infinite
mercy, though we can be quite stingy in doling it out. The Old Testa-
ment speaks of "God's deliverance," but I suppose this is only pos-
sible if God can also abandon. There's the problem. You can't have it
both ways. God cannot deliver unless God can also abandon. I don't
believe in deliverance because I don't believe in abandonment. God
sustains, not delivers. God "delivers us" in sustenance, in carrying us
through tough times, not by ending them. It's how "Big Big" adores.

In the face of this adoring God, we are like fish in the ocean . . .
looking for the ocean. God is forever screaming at us: "You ARE in
the ocean." We get stuck sometimes in praying to prove something
or acquire something. It is never enough until we lose ourselves in
loving. Then we can see that this is what God's adoring is leading us
toward anyway. Part of our stuck-ness is thinking that resting in God

is our goal, but it is the very generosity of God that points away from God to loving. Nothing is separate from the Holy One and nothing is meant to separate us from each other.

Yo-Yo Ma says that when he plays the cello, he's not trying to prove something; he's trying to share something. Meister Eckhart invites us to the "virgin mind," like the Buddhists' "beginner's mind." We train our mind to be still and not empty. We seek to be steady and aspire to an evenness. We clear the deck and find the generosity of God in those touchstones, the moments when we are quickened to become the generosity of God in the world. We ponder carefully those moments where there is a quickening. It's not our rest stop, but our departure point. Like the mystic Brother Lawrence who sees a tree, but *really sees* it. For him it becomes a singular moment of God. This quickening never left him.

On a recent flight home from Denver with two homegirls, Rosemary and Gennell, I sit in my usual place on Southwest, exit row, aisle. They scoot into the row ahead of me so they can peer out the window. I am writing furiously in preparation for a big talk the next day. We are near landing and I can see the tops of the homegirls' heads, now with their hoods on. Rosemary is leaning on Gennell, either sleeping or looking out the window. Just the sight of them fills me with a "Brother Lawrence quickening." My eyes fill with tears, and I see the fullness I was meant to see. I am taken over by this complete love for these two women, holding all they've had to carry, with a boundless admiration. Merton says that "once in a while, you cross over into God." Not a rest stop, but always a departure point.

After communion at Juvenile Hall, I distribute my card to all the homies gathered there. I do my usual riff. I tell them about all the heavily tattooed gang members who walk into my office after years in prison and ask, "Remember me?" More often than not, after all these many years, I don't. "You baptized me." I brighten as he fishes out the card I gave him right after that sacrament. I study the wrinkled, yellowing card and tell him that we haven't been at that location in more than twenty years. I hand the card back and now he's tearing up. "I shoulda called you." I tell this story almost always after passing out my card at the end of mass at Juvenile Hall.

"Don't be that guy," I tell them. "Call me when you get out."

When the mass is over, the kids start to file out to return to their units. I'm shaking each hand. One kid holds up the card I had given him just minutes before and waxes nostalgic. "Back in 2020, Father Greg Boyle handed me a card just like this."

I look at him and say, "And he just handed it to you again in 2023."

He grows pie-eyed incredulous. "No . . . wait . . . you're Father Greg?" In a sense, we're always being handed the invitation. It is our constant rendezvous with this God, endlessly extending God's self, that awakens us. We quicken and say, "No . . . wait."

With a newly embraced mystical vision, we follow the mystical teacher, Jesus. The goal of all mystical teachers is to awaken. We are being asked to see everything anew all the time. Theologian Megan McKenna writes that "God is not impartial." Not sure what that means. I suppose it wants us to know that "God hears the cry of the poor." Yes, indeed. But this Tender One doesn't draw lines. She erases them.

We are all woven together in this divine fabric. The "quickenings" come and go, but still we find rest in the plenitude of God, lodged in every damn thing. Once in a while, we do cross over into God. This Wild God is infinitely loving and trying to access us. Find the invitation. Feel God trying to get the perfect photo. Our practice wants to calibrate our hearts to a habituated sensitivity where we find our-selves floating in this luminous ocean and we abide there with joy. We ARE in the ocean. We discover, in this abiding, that we each are an utterly unique capacity to bring this Wild God into the world. Just as deftly, we can produce a still-warm burrito, the special kind, for each other. We ARE the sustenance of God. Just . . . forth.

2

THE CRUELTY POINTS

SITTING IN THE CHICAGO-MIDWAY AIRPORT, I SAW A YOUNG woman with a T-shirt that said boldly, "Love Not Hate." It was around the time after a disturbed man had attacked an elderly Asian woman on a street in San Francisco. (*New York Times*: "Man Hit Woman 125 Times Because She Was Asian, Officials Say." Still, I'm going with mental illness.) I thought to myself that if I wore that shirt, it would be all about me and MY stance on the issue. It doesn't announce a message so much as spotlight me. It can't be about me. I saw her and I didn't think to nod, or say, "Yes," or signal a thumbs-up of approval. Instead, I immediately thought, *THAT is why we don't make progress.* My reaction surprised me. I spent time with it. I could see that the T-shirt still creates the "Other." (Another time, another T-shirt: "Racist People Suck." Same thing.) It says, in no uncertain terms, "I belong to those who love . . . AND I stand against those who hate." The "othering" is the opposite of who God is. It says that there are some folks who don't belong to us, or they will belong only if they change their behavior. Later, in the same airport, I saw an older woman wearing a sweatshirt that said in huge, black letters, "UNWELL." And I think, *YES...finally...progress.*

None of us are healed until all of us are healed. And all of us, to some degree, are not fully whole. I'm certainly not. But surely no one who is well hates.

Matthew Dowd, a political commentator, asks why did it take one hundred years from the end of Reconstruction to Emmett Till? He suggests that the answer is because one-third of the American people did not believe that all men and women are created equal. He further asks: Why did it take some sixty years from Martin Luther King, Jr., the Civil Rights Act, and the Voting Rights Act to Donald Trump? He again posits that it is because one-third of the American people do not believe that all men and women are created equal. Let's say he's correct. Then who are those people?

Before we address that question, I want to propose that, with reverence, we can overthrow the tyranny of our judgments and watch as a more available and tender heart appears. It IS possible to cultivate the ability to exist with anguish and pain without having to control or change it. We try to welcome whatever opens our being to the shared pain of the world. It is our God-given curiosity that makes judgment impossible. It opens the door to wanting more information. It becomes slow to the draw. Who are these people who do not believe that all men and women are created equal? Judgment is kept waiting in the hallway while we lean in with curiosity. We lean with kind attention filled with awe and patience. It is a humble leaning that swats away certainty. It wants to know "what is," with a shame-free and robust acceptance. Truth be told, you never have to let judgment into the room at all.

Who are these people? Are they simply bad people? Are they merely ignorant? If we assume so, nothing is illuminated. Can anyone be well, whole, and healthy and believe that all men and women are not created equal? I don't think so. They hold this belief not because they are cruel, but because they are strangers to themselves. That is not a value judgment, but a health assessment. For nothing can touch anyone's goodness, not even holding such a view. Goodness and belonging remain intact, no matter what unhealthy notion we find ourselves clinging to.

Where do our nation's racial hypocrisy and autocratic leanings come from? How we answer that question will set us on a path. If we blame ignorance, we redouble our efforts to win the argument. We infuse the information and increase the education. If we blame hatred, we shake our fist with moral indignation and incessantly wag our fingers. We will grow breathless insisting people do good and avoid evil. But perhaps the moment comes when we compassionately surmise that we need to gently accompany each other toward a more whole sense of well-being. Ilia Delio calls the effort "becoming wholemakers." "That you may be whole, as your Heavenly Father is whole." We'll get there.

An excellent book of searing essays is *The Cruelty Is The Point* by Adam Serwer. It underscores quite horrific moments in these recent years, with great historic reach, and comes to the conclusion that "the cruelty is the point." Just recently, for example, the governor of Texas mentioned in a tweet that the victims of a terrible mass shooting were "illegal immigrants." A political commentator on TV, reflecting on this tweet, concluded his remarks with "Once again, the cruelty is the point." It has become a shorthand phrase to explain "bad people doing bad things."

In forty years of working with gang members in Los Angeles, I'm familiar with this shorthand. I think we can only be certain of this: It isn't that "the cruelty is the point" but, rather, that "the cruelty . . . points." It points beyond itself to things that indeed need our attention. It points to mental anguish, wounds, damage, and trauma that need our healing. Does the cruelty always point to such things? Yes. No exceptions. Accompanying gang members has taught me this.

A bad diagnosis can't ever lead us to a good treatment plan. It matters how we name things. Asserting that the cruelty is the point doesn't refine our moral compass, because its wheels are spinning too much in moral outrage. The measure of our resolve lies not in the size of our denunciation, but in our willingness to get underneath things. Kanye West sends an anti-Semitic tweet. "Anti-Semitic" describes it. Mental illness explains it. Of course, we don't like explanations because they feel like excuses, and, worse, they take the air out of our denunciation. But explanations don't excuse.

In the face of senseless gun violence, political treachery and revenge, hate crimes, mass shootings, and terrorist attacks, some people will just say, "Sin and evil are on display." When we do this, we've given up. We're not even trying. We declare that we will no longer be seeking solutions, because we believe that human beings are somehow stained from the start. Original sin doesn't explain the terrible. Lots of things do. Original sin is not one of them. There is no sin gene in us. We're born from love and always invited to love. The Incarnation gives flesh to God; then we participate in this "wholemaking," divine love. We seek out the transcendent, inclusive, and life-giving impulse within. We are born for this.

In a packed church hall, responding to a question, I told the audience, "I've never met anyone evil . . . and neither have you."

Then an elderly gentleman in the front row yells out, "Trust me, I have." The audience laughed. I left it at that, but I thought, *No, you haven't; you only think you did.* We've all met the broken, the despondent and damaged, the desperate and unwell, the traumatized, wounded, and injured. But never anybody evil. Buddhists see suffering where Western Christians may only see sin. We are all broken, and knowing that helps us recognize it everywhere. And further, it blossoms into compassionate love.

I asked a friend to talk to her daughter who had just graduated from a Jesuit university about how she and her peers saw sin. Her daughter said, "We don't really use the word 'sin' or talk about it. Sin is an Old World map." Now, I suppose some might lament that sin is not on the front burner. It's actually not even on the back burner. It is nowhere near the stove. And, of course, if you tried to use an Old World map today to get you to, say, Iraq, it would drop you off at Mesopotamia.

We could lament that young folks might see sin this way. Or we could find the invitation in it. Is the God of love looking down on a sinful world in need of salvation, or does our God see a broken world in pain and in need of healing? Scripture has it as "Then your light shall break like the dawn and your wound shall quickly be healed. The light shall rise for you in your gloom. The darkness shall become for you like midday." I endlessly tell gang members that the God of love doesn't see sin. Our God sees son (and daughter). "I believe that sin has no substance," Julian of Norwich writes, "not a particle of being." Then she says, "With all due respect to Mother Church . . . but this does not line up." She couldn't get sin to align with her God of love.

Jesus asks the demoniac who is terrorizing the neighbors, writing on walls, selling drugs, shooting at people, harassing folks as they walk by, "What is your name?"

The guy says, "Legion," which at first bounce means, "There are a lot of my homies to back me up." But the word actually means "I am what has afflicted me." The invitation and plea is for healing. And Jesus does. Even though it would appear he "drives out the demon," he's actually freeing him of his affliction and asking him not to define himself this way anymore. More liberation than salvation. The demoniac's "growth" is not about becoming less sinful, but more joyful. He is now connected to a community, having been liberated from his isolation. Jesus has made him whole. We do the same. And we begin by acknowledging that the demoniac's illness and lack of brain health is nothing he chose. It chose him.

Many years ago, at a huge Jesuit gathering, one Jesuit in particular was highlighted for his extraordinary generosity. He was invited to stand. He had apparently agreed to be sent to our version of Siberia to minister to the Siberians there. The Jesuit at the microphone, pointing at the man standing, pronounced, "Now THAT is a good Jesuit." I winced. I knew that a "good Jesuit" could not exist unless there was a "bad Jesuit." I knew that was impossible. Over fifty years as a Jesuit, I've never met a bad one. I've met many broken Jesuits: traumatized; despondent; on the spectrum; wounded; stuck in shame, mental illness, and crippling inferiority. I've known Jesuits who are strangers to themselves. But I've never met a bad one. Please don't call me a good one.

Jesus didn't condemn the woman involved in the sex trade who was washing his feet. He knew her pure heart. He could see the preciousness of her soul. The "good" folks watching it all were full of judgment. They were self-serving and flush with pride. Not bad guys; they just hadn't been properly introduced to themselves yet. Truth be told, they were self-absorbed. And, worse, self-assertive. Because we are human, our natural resting place is distracted self-absorption. What the adherents to Baha'i call "the insistent self." "I'm worried about me." "I wonder about me." "I'm anxious about me."

At another airport, another woman was wearing a sweatshirt that had on it some phrase in tiny print. I had to move close enough to read it. I was soon startled by what was written in the smallest of fonts: "Don't fuck with my energy." Choosing to be humble and kind is part of our practice that doesn't mess with anyone's energy. Like the loving awareness that chooses to "wash feet" and serve, it unites what is scattered. It attaches what has been severed. All mystics know to step outside themselves and focus on the other. That's where the joy is. Joy is the other side of our self-absorption. People get diverted, like the dog who spots the squirrel. People aren't unkind, just distracted.

I'm at the ATM on Christmas Eve. I can hear a woman in the parking lot of the Wells Fargo speaking loudly, with great agitation, into her cell phone. It becomes clear that she is talking to the police. "I just don't want my kids to see this." I turn the corner, walk past the woman, and see what she wants shielded from her kids. Down half a block, there's a middle-aged Black man without a stitch of clothing. He's trembling, clearly terrified that he finds himself naked, standing at the corner of Indiana and Whittier. The cops are on their way. One hopes he'll get the help he needs. He belongs to us. No one well gets butt-naked and stands outside the ATM on Christmas Eve.

We are all familiar with the post-9/11 mantra "See Something. Say Something." Riding a train in London, headed to Heathrow Airport, I notice a similar warning, but with something additional. The poster says, "See it. Say it. Sort it." They explain further that if you see something, say something, and then "We will sort it out." This third step is helpful and perhaps a good corrective to our American version. It acknowledges that things NEED to be sorted out together. Sometimes a naked man at Whittier and Indiana on Christmas Eve is not just a cavalier lawbreaker. We need to sort it.

Part of our sorting is not just naming things correctly, but finding the right questions to ask. Consider the Zen concept of *Mu*. When one is asked a yes-or-no question, you "Mu." Which is to say, un-ask that question. Find another question or ask it in another way.

Before I was ordained, I was teaching at my alma mater, Loyola High School in Los Angeles. In the early morning, before classes begin, I hear the phone ringing in my bedroom. I race to it and it's my oldest sister, Eileen, telling me that her husband, Edgar, is driving home and he's been hearing voices on the radio telling him to kill her and their two young boys, Eddie and Kevin. I ask a fellow Jesuit, Art Encinas, to take over my class and I hurry to Pasadena, help pack them all up, and drop them off at my parents' house. After a time of separation, they divorced and my sister forged a new life with her boys. She eventually married Michael, with whom she has shared a life for forty years.

Edgar, my former brother-in-law, was gripped by a mental illness inherited from his father. As the years progressed, both his sons fell into a similar mental anguish, not of their choosing. The younger of the two, Kevin, well into his thirties, had taken to lying down in the back of my sister's car so as not to be seen by "the men" following them. One Sunday I sat him down in my sister's home, and sweet, gentle Kevin agreed to see a professional the next day.

When I woke the following morning, I had two messages. One

from Kevin: "Uncle Greg. I need to talk to you. Call me as soon as you can. Love you." The next one from Eileen, screaming: "Kevin has hung himself in the basement." He left a suicide note: "I'm sorry I did this. If I didn't, they would have killed Uncle Greg."

Eight years later, Eddie was found hanging in his office in Singapore. Prior to this, he had spent years doing all manner of self-medicating. His pain followed him everywhere he went. Find another question. Or ask it in another way. Neither of my nephews chose their anguish. It chose them.

Martin Luther King writes: "Darkness cannot drive out darkness, only light can do that. Hate cannot drive out hate, only love can do that." But what if hate is not what we think it is? What if hate is not something you drive out, but something you heal? Hate is an indicator. Gang members, before healing happens, are filled with hate for rival, enemy gang members, sometimes parents, and often "baby mamas." The hate is never about conflict, nor is it rational. It indicates a lack of health. Indeed, love heals, but it does not drive out hate. After a greatly contested election in Ohio, I was driving there and saw a billboard: "Stop Hating Each Other Because You Disagree." But hatred is about health, not disagreement.

People often call legislators cowards for refusing to do something sensible on gun safety. Equally, people will call gunmen involved in mass killings cowards as well. It would be more accurate to say that a great many legislators are not healthy enough to be courageous. Otherwise, we think the problem is character rather than health, and moral depravity rather than true sickness.

I've never seen anyone reject love. People get stuck in despair, their own trauma, and severe mental anguish. But humans aren't inclined to reject love. Sometimes, they need to heal just enough to give it access. The Eastern Orthodox mindset thinks Westerners are too pessimistic. The sin gene. It's not so much that humans choose badly, but there is so much that can color our choices. The ego has such a capacity for self-deception. We are all on a continuum of health.

We can cite January 6 as an example. There is a spectrum of poor health on display. On one end, there is the guy in his recliner watching the insurrection on TV from San Bernardino and cheering the mob on. At the other end is the shirtless gentleman in the horned fur hat. In the middle of the spectrum is the LAPD officer who flew to DC to attend the Stop the Steal rally, but was quick to tell superiors, "I went straight to my hotel room right after." None of this has to do with politics or policy or partisanship. None of this has to do with goodness or intelligence. Are we fully well and healthy, cheering on a mob, storming the capitol, attending a Stop the Steal rally, or dressed in a horned fur hat at the speaker of the house's chair? What we know for sure is that every single one of these folks is unshakably good and belongs to us. How can we choose to be curious about wounds that lie underneath this delusion? Our narratives need revising. Healing is in order and compassion is required. If we could see the secret history of each person, it would surely disarm our hearts.

Donald Trump says of the January 6 folks: "They were mostly good people." I would disagree. They were all good. Barack Obama and Trevor Noah discuss racism in America. Obama asserts: "Most of the American people are good people." Again, I have to disagree. All are unshakably good. What doesn't touch their goodness is their brain health. For no one healthy storms the capitol or is a racist. Jen Psaki comments on Trump's provocative language: "There's a market for the tyranny he's selling." Perhaps. But surely no one healthy longs for tyranny. We draw the lines in ways that are not helpful: good/

bad, stupid/smart. What seems closer to God's take: healed or not so much.

Lots of Buddhist teachers will speak of our "basic goodness," others, "inherent goodness," still others "essential goodness." I've never much liked these phrases. It feels tentative, and "basic," "essential," and "inherent" all seem to hedge our bets. These notions suggest that our goodness is something we can abandon. It feels more aligned with the heart of God to suggest that we don't always see our unshakable goodness so clearly. Buddhists speak of the dust covering our eyes. Is it true that we ignore, abandon, or reject our goodness? Perhaps it is more accurate to say that despair, trauma, mental anguish, and plain old distraction can block our view of our goodness. But if we see it clearly, watch what happens. God only sees goodness and wants us to see what God sees.

Eknath Easwaran says, "Original goodness . . . is our real nature." Warmer. I say *unshakable* goodness, because I don't think we should allow wiggle room. We want to give our goodness its undeniable place at the center of our truth. We don't have the potential for goodness as we might have for artistic accomplishment. Even if it's the "little spark" of which Eckhart speaks, it is the pilot light of true goodness waiting to peel away all that covers it from our view so it can burn brightly. Darkness becoming midday. Unshakable goodness IS who God knows us to be.

The tattoo "Trust No One" is prominently displayed on Byron's neck. It's not uncommon to see this phrase featured on a homie's skin. I always wonder: What does it announce? That the homie is savvy or injured? Jack Kornfield says, "Sometimes it's your loving heart that opens your broken heart." Indeed, gang members can make idols of their shame and disgrace, having been strafed with messages of blame, guilt, and constant threats of punishment. The truth is, it's the loving heart that God sees. Once a homie catches sight of it, the "little spark" ignites a bit.

Byron was telling me about the time a police squad car was following him home once he got off the freeway. The police car trails Byron right into his driveway and parks behind him. The cop asks him, "Do you live here?" He answers, "Why wouldn't I live here?" I suggest that maybe a simple "yes" would have been more helpful. This apparently illustrates Byron's distrustful stance in the world. In the HR office: "Why wouldn't I have my vaccination card?" With a waitress: "Why wouldn't I want ranch dressing?" This catchphrase fuels no end of kidding, "capping on him," from those who know him.

One day, Byron comes to my office with a gift: an Albert Einstein bobblehead. I'm visibly perplexed by this present. Byron explains: "'Cuz you're the smartest man I know . . . it's metaphorical." True enough, Byron is the song God sings. In the elasticity of his tender heart, he can move beyond distrust and free-fall into his own indisputable goodness. Sometimes the most difficult stranger to welcome is the one inside of us.

Cradling the small box holding the "metaphorical" Albert Einstein bobblehead, I look at Byron and say, "Why wouldn't I be proud to call you my son?"

Drug addicts and gang members are neither helplessly subject to irresistible impulses or making totally free decisions. Judgment hasn't been obliterated but impaired. Their capacity to choose gets compromised. People who get addicted (and join gangs) have other psychiatric disorders, traumatic childhoods, or both. Seventy-five percent of women addicted to heroin were sexually abused as children. As we develop and grow, we gain more control and can optimize our ability to choose. Experts contend that distorted thinking is more important in addictive behavior than an overwhelming desire to get high. The homie who feels despondent, who regularly beats himself up and can conjure up no viable image of tomorrow, is more influenced by his inner suffering than by the lure to gangbang (to be active in gang activity) or how good this drug makes you feel. We already know who is more likely to join a gang or slide into to addiction and, consequently, we know what will accelerate recovery. So we address poverty, despair, trauma, and mental health. Everyone has agency, but many circumstances can compromise that. We can compassionately hold folks responsible while offering a therapeutic way out of this wilderness. Comfort and purpose feel out of reach for the gang member. This hurting despair drives gangbanging more than the thrill of some adrenaline rush.

Health and illness are surely on a continuum, a spectrum of severity. And none of it has to do with morality. If we believe that our home is each other in love, then healthy people can, for example, forgive. People who aren't well can't. The moral overlay doesn't add anything. If we create therapeutic communities and we all participate in "whole-making," then we help each other move forward, not "get over" their pain, but put one foot in front of the next. You don't "move on" from trauma but learn to move with it. Being cherished helps you integrate your traumatic memories so they can become less dissociating. We are invited to help each other do this. If we could heal those things that compromise agency, people would settle into health.

The moral quest has never kept us moral; it's just kept us from each other. So maybe we should abandon the moral quest, since it's an Old World map, and embrace instead the journey to wholeness, flourishing love, and defiant joy. We don't want to end up in Meso-potamia. Yes, we want to do the next right thing, but what is the next right thing and who is able to choose it? Only the healthy person can. So we help each other, not to make better choices but to walk home to well-being and deeper growth in love. Cherishing leads us to this warm embrace of the journey to wholeness.

Moises wants back into Homeboy. It's been three months since he was told, "Come back when you're ready." Readiness in his case means rehab. He can't stop drinking. I suspect he thinks I've forgotten about the invitation to get clean. "Son, what happened to your illness?"

He seems genuinely perplexed, "What illness?"

I lean in. "*Mijito de mi cora*, what is your illness?"

He searches: "I make bad choices?"

I lean in even further, "Son . . . what . . . is your illness?"

He pauses, "I make . . . REALLY bad choices?" No. It's not about Moises making better choices but allowing himself to reside in the next healthy step to take.

Moises left me a voicemail message once: "Call me at your in-convenience." So I did. He was inflamed. As they say, some "baby mama drama." He was on the very ledge of danger and some vague, ill-advised action. He was "putting a 10 on it." The homies say this when someone, like Moises, is hyper-exaggerating. I caution him a bit and he tells me: "If I'm lying, may God throw the first stone." When we wind down the conversation, he says, "I never should have called you. You always be calmin' my stupid ass down."

The Anti-Defamation League created a recent ad about standing up to Jewish hate. A father and his teenage son are driving a truck in the pouring rain. The father stops the car and says, "I saw what you've been posting." The son squirms. "Hitler was right?" Again the son is clearly uncomfortable and looks straight ahead. "I didn't teach you that," his father says. "You hide behind your screen," he continues, "spewing all this hatred and ugliness. You got something you want to say? Get out of the truck and say it to their faces." The father points as the windshield wipers reveal that they are now parked in front of a synagogue as young families with children are leaving the service, holding umbrellas, laughing and dodging puddles. The son is speechless, and his discomfort is palpable. Then the father gently places his hand on the boy's cheek. The screen goes dark and it says, "'Hitler was right'" was posted over 70,000 times last year. There's no looking away from hate." It's an effective ad, but the most powerful, illuminating moment is the touch, the hand on the cheek. Any healthy parent would know that this kid is in trouble. His posting . . . points. Does the boy need "counter-messaging"? Is this about morality or does the "hate" indicate something else that needs our attention? Clearly, the answer is not about changing his mind, but healing his wound. There is no looking away from hate, but what if hate is not what we think it is? Do we "stand up to it" or do we get underneath it, so it can be healed? Is white supremacy an ideology or an illness?

No one healthy thinks Israel has no right to exist. No one healed thinks Hamas doesn't belong to us. No one well thinks Palestinians shouldn't be free. No one whole says, "From the river to the sea." We are constantly bombarded with dehumanizing messages on all sides of all issues. This is undeniably an unnecessary exercise. We can always point things out, but we want to point the way. We don't want to settle for describing problems; we want to hold out for explanations. We don't have enemies; we have injuries. We don't have hate; we have wounds. We don't have fear; we have the shared ruin of our common, human brokenness. Everyone belongs and everyone's good.

After one of the many mass shootings in our country's recent history, a bishop declared, "Sacred Scripture clearly says that God stands with the victims and not the victimizers." I am almost certain this bishop could "proof text" that statement and cite chapter and verse in "Sacred Scripture," but just as certainly, he could never align this assertion with the heart of the God of love. Scripture is inspired and imperfect. It is always doing the best it can. To be clear: "Us and Them" language is the opposite view of the God we actually have. God doesn't see "victims and victimizers" but only ever sons and daughters. When we "want justice," it ought never to be about vengeance or punishment. God just wants us to be whole. There's justice for you. So, with God, we try and restore the wholeness. We mend the severed belonging. God manages to see underneath everything to find the wound that needs love and healing. Victim and victimizer. God's love can walk and chew gum at the same time.

The Gospel challenge is to find room in our hearts for everybody. Everybody. We get tripped up on our moral outrage, unable to plow through it and land on a moral compass. A homie acts inappropriately with women at Homeboy. It's a tough problem. How do we proceed in actually helping him, keeping at bay cries of "Off with his head," steering clear of demonizing while at the same time, not only keeping the place actually safe for women, but also ensuring that they *feel* safe? The Gospel invites us to make room in our hearts for these women and this man. Humans generally don't like this idea, but Jesus does. You watch the Parkland shooter plead guilty and Jesus knows that there is room in our spacious hearts for everybody. He is given a sentence of life without the possibility of parole instead of the death penalty, and, still, Jesus has room. Making room does not push out the victims and their families.

Where we start will indicate where we all end up. Nobody vs. Anybody is God's dream come true. We work and walk toward that. They asked Abraham Lincoln about his religious beliefs: "When I do good, I feel good. When I do bad, I feel bad. And that's my religion." And certainly, no unhealthy and disordered impulse can ever touch one's goodness or one's secure place in belonging. All cruelty points to the wound in need of healing. We make progress when we walk each other home to this wholeness.

Camila has worked at Homeboy off and on for many years. Because of very weighty mental health issues and sporadic meth use, she wanders away from us, will do a stint in jail or prison, and yet always return. Homeboy is more home than home. On occasion, we need to put her on the "no-fly list." People will say, "We're starting to get 'BAD' Camila." Everyone knows what this means. She's off her meds and using meth and it's all a matter of time. The outburst will arrive. We've had many. Sometimes we have to call the police. We love her so much that we *have* to call the police. We adore Camila so much that we can't let her into the building. Our love is clear. Once she kicked in the front door. Shattered glass everywhere. Camila doesn't have a grievance. She needs to be stopped, not punished. Her action was not a "hate crime." Though it was hugely annoying, I didn't take it personally, nor, for even a second, did I think this vandalism touched her goodness or jeopardized her belonging to us. She's not well and we will only point her toward her own health and do everything we can to lovingly help her get there.

We live in a wounded and wounding world. And loving the wounded is never a wasted effort. Only love makes progress. But fear and negativity keep us stuck. Demonizing and dehumanizing end all conversations and shut down our hope for progress. We all know Camila beyond the outrageous behavior. She's not good one day and bad the next. At times she's well, and other times, not so much. That's all. We stay as close as we can to the love that knows no bounds. We're trying to create a belonging community, not a behaving one. Finally, progress.

But if we are stuck in moral outrage, we demonize and shake our fists at people, denouncing at our fullest volume. We always tinker with our narratives so that they remain true. And, surely, other people's "demons" are easier to contend with than our own. It helps to know our truth, inhabit it, and make sure we are not strangers to ourselves. Our true compass frees us to be compassionate, to love folks into their wholeness. It keeps us focused only on their health. Now we can strive to repair and restore what is severed. Not to call people out, but to call them in and invite them to their own well-being. That's a good treatment plan, born of a good diagnosis. A tender hand on a cheek, rather than winning the argument and replacing one message with another.

Take conspiracy theories. Nearly every conspiracy theory is rooted in a "secret cabal" that runs everything. John Birchers saw Commies. QAnon sees pedophile Democrats. The truth is no healthy person spreads disinformation. And no healthy person buys it. It is all a measure of health.

A pastor was lamenting that many of his parishioners bought into the QAnon conspiracies. "Good people were taken in by this stuff," he said. But what does goodness have to do with it? The *New Yorker* examines why people join cults. It essentially asks, "Why would a normal woman join that cult?" The very question departs from the same and incorrect starting point: the idea of a "normal," rational actor coming from a healthy place. We assume everything is rational, motive-driven, and I suspect it rarely is.

Think of the action required of you to gain admission into hell. Now think of how ill you'd have to be to meet that requirement. No one healthy has ever killed children in a classroom. No one well has ever invaded Ukraine. No one whole has ever slapped Chris Rock at the Oscars. Spokesman for the State Department John Kirby is asked if Putin is a rational actor. "I can't talk to his psychology," he says, "but I think we can all speak to his depravity." But "depravity" describes and psychology explains. And if you exhibit "depravity," you are not well.

I'm giving a talk at Lakeside Chautauqua, outside at this bandstand overlooking the lake. Periodically, I can see that near this one tree, birds are attacking people. This describes it. But later I learn that the birds are frightened and are protecting their nests. This explains it. After this talk, a man asks how he can get beyond the trauma, PTSD, and resentment he feels toward a young Black man, a stranger, who terrorized him and his wife in Cleveland. I say, "Mental illness is tough and challenging for all of us."

He turns testy: "I don't think he was mentally ill at all. I think he just gets off on terrifying old white couples." *Mu.*

So I say, "Let me phrase the question differently. Does a healthy, whole, well person . . . ever get off terrifying old white couples?"

Recently, I was reading a moral theologian who wrote that "sin is the failure to bother to love." Who, exactly, are those who don't bother to love? Not bad people, nor people leading with the badness folks claim is in each of us, but, rather, the distracted, the self-absorbed, the traumatized, the despondent, and those in a constant struggle with mental anguish. What we have here is not a failure to bother to love, but a whole world of things that block our capacity to love. If it becomes too painful to be ourselves, we languish in a disconnected stupor. Only a cherishing compassion can jostle us from it.

My friend, Mary, is a mystic. She's also a grandmother who has a few years on me and lives alone in a tiny apartment in San Francisco. She is much like Julian of Norwich, an anchorite, dedicated to prayer and quite attuned to "God's presencing God's self" in her life. While recuperating from knee surgery, she went out for a walk, and she saw a woman in her twenties, who was quite disheveled and clearly hadn't bathed in a while, leaning for ballast against a USPS mailbox. She had on one flip-flop, and the other foot was swollen and discolored. It was a biting-cold and windy day. Mary tells me that the woman "is yelling at the universe. And in a world of her own." Mary wanted to connect to her, but she had nothing—no money, no food, none of the clean socks that she often carried in her purse. But she carried no purse today. So she kept walking. She walked nearly a block farther, then turned around and came back. She asked the woman, "Is Fillmore Street in this direction?" Mary knew exactly where Fillmore Street was. Mary tells me that the "woman came to complete stillness and saw me and knew everything necessary about me. We were in the same world." The woman said yes, then hesitated a bit, saying she thought so. Mary thanked her and said she'd give it a try. As she told me, "We were looking right at each other in the eye. The stillness was in control." Mary thanked her again and walked away in that direction. She listened until she was out of earshot and she heard no more screaming. Mary is quick to tell me, "This was no cure." She reflects on what she'd give folks from now on, along with cash, food, and socks. She'd ask people directions. "Because in these few seconds, perhaps one minute total, the woman was composed and calm. Because

I asked for knowledge, the woman, for a moment, felt noble." This discovery made Mary cry in the telling of it. The hidden wholeness seen and coaxed out of its hiding place. "To those in darkness, show yourselves."

Saint Francis of Assisi had a leper phobia. He was terrified of them. I suspect he found himself clinging to an understandable concern of infection. One day, he saw a leper, got off his horse, and, I suppose, "asked him for directions." He saw the leper and he saw Jesus. They "showed themselves" to each other. Saint Francis kissed the leper and never saw another as "other" again. The mystical tradition is to treat every guest as God. Hagar writes: "You are the God who sees me." The stillness is in control. Everyone is seen.

Isaac the Syrian, who died in AD 700, said that the Incarnation is not about sin. It's about the love of God needing to become tender. With cherishing compassion, the world just stops in its tracks; the stillness takes over. We realize that the truly thrilling thing happening in our midst is tenderness. Love provides the explanation for the Incarnation. Not sin. Tenderness asks for directions.

I didn't hear this story until thirteen years after the fact. I took José and Andres to help me speak to six hundred social workers in Richmond, Virginia. José, who is Latino, and Andres, who is Black, are from enemy gangs. Some hours after dinner, they feel hungry again and wander out beyond our hotel.

The two of them find a Hardee's, walk in, and see they are the only customers there. Two men and one woman, all white, are working behind the counter. The three of them are laughing and carrying on until José and Andres walk up, and then they go silent. José orders a burger, and the guy behind the counter tells him, "We don't serve rice and beans here."

José, a tad oblivious, says, "That's okay. I'd like a cheeseburger."

The guy continues, "There's not one tortilla in this whole place."

Again José says, "I don't want a tortilla, just a cheeseburger."

Andres comes to his aid. "Come on, man, he just wants a cheeseburger."

The guy turns to Andres and says, "We don't got no watermelon, either." Now the chill sets in and Andres signals to José that maybe it's best to leave.

I'm not sure why it took thirteen years before José told me that story. Maybe when you're shamed, you embody the shame. No one well, whole, or healthy treats human beings this way. Racism describes this, but impairment in brain health explains it.

In an article I read, the author asked, "If we imagined racism as a spiritual problem, how might that shift the ways we choose to grapple with it?" But if we imagined racism as a mental health issue, then it allows for both compassion and a solution. I suspect the singular reason we don't make progress is that we have never seen this as a mental health issue, but a moral one.

We always get tripped up when we say "mental illness" because we think it has to require some diagnosis in order to qualify. Perhaps it's more palatable to say that no one healthy does this. On October 1, 2017, a sixty-four-year-old man shot from the thirty-second floor of the Mandalay Bay Resort and Casino in Las Vegas. He fired 1,000 bullets, killed 60 people, and injured 413 others. The ensuing panic injured another 450 people. I knew folks who were at that concert and still suffer from the trauma of it.

A year later, very frustrated detectives closed the case because they "could not determine a motive." They ruled out mental illness because they couldn't find any psychiatrist with a file on this man. They couldn't locate a "diagnosis" anywhere. Speaking before a hotel ball-room filled with psychiatrists, I asked them rhetorically to imagine a motive since the police couldn't find one. Did his wife leave him? Did she leave him for his best friend? Did he get fired? Doesn't matter. Whatever you can conjure as a motive, nothing meets this horror. I posited that no healthy person has ever done such a thing. The psychiatrists were upset with me. They thought such talk stigmatizes the mentally ill. Call me new-fashioned: I think it helps to talk about stuff. I also told them that I hoped it goes without saying that not all diagnosed, mentally anguished people would ever commit such a horror. But, equally, it goes without saying that no one whole has ever perpetrated a tragedy like this, either. Still, they are unshakably good and belong to us. Explaining is not excusing. It's how we make progress.

There was a story in the *Los Angeles Times* about a young man from the gang MS-13. He was homeless, living in a tent. He robbed a man, killed him, and threw his body over a cliff. His probation officer said, "Maybe he had mental health issues, but mainly he was committed to hate." Again, I think we can eliminate the "committed to hate" part. We rewind the tape, and now we extend ourselves to the broken young man living in a tent. "Talking him out of hate" needs to seem to us as futile and unsophisticated. How can we heal wounds in a timely way, before society insists on punishing them?

Eddie Glaude, Jr., in a conversation on Nicolle Wallace's show, cautions her with great passion about speaking of Trump followers: "They're not kooks. They're dangerous." Of course, I've known many dangerous "kooks" in my lifetime. As they say, "A clown with a flamethrower . . . still has a flamethrower."

We try to address policing, for example, and we might underscore how it is a systemic problem. Many others have addressed the pervasive culture in law enforcement that sees their mandate more as "warrior" than "public servant." Still others might emphasize the need to "weed out the bad apples." Yet, if we think it's about bad apples, we're in the wrong orchard. Enlightened chiefs of police will tell their officers, "Remember, today you will encounter people having the worst day of their lives." The rise in hate crimes, suicides, fentanyl overdoses, and police using excessive force would seem to undeniably point to that and beyond.

Last example. I promise. A man wielding a heavy chain with a padlock at the end of it smashes the window of a Burlington store in the Valley. He assaults two women inside. The police are called. They shoot him. They use deadly force (though it seems they could have easily subdued him without it) because he has established himself as "a bad guy." The man didn't have a gun. One of the bullets that the police discharged bounced off the floor, ricocheted off a wall, and killed a fourteen-year-old girl trying on a quinceañera dress in the dressing room. She died in her mother's arms. It was tragic and horrific, and certainly, the police felt terrible about this unspeakable loss of life. The *LA Times* included this one lone sentence, sitting all by itself in the article, not connected to any other paragraph: "It's unclear whether the suspect in the Burlington case had mental issues." I put the paper down. *Unclear to whom?* I asked myself. No rational, healthy, well, nearly whole human has ever done this in the history of the world. No man, woman, or child is unclear about this.

Justice can never be about vengeance or punishment. God just wants us to be whole, and so we join God in that undertaking. We try and restore wholeness. The Blackfeet tribe believed that bad deeds happened when people felt outside the family. Justice was bringing them back in. Experts will say that studies show that there are fewer violent crimes when the chances of being caught and punished are high. This threat is a deterrence for healthy people who don't need to be deterred. But for those who are broken and estranged from themselves, deterrence falls on their deaf ears. Not because they're bad, but because their agency is too compromised to receive the warning.

Only healing reduces crime. A police officer in the country said once, "I don't believe in the electric chair, I believe in the electric bleachers." We think that punishment will usher in repair and justice. Our starting point is that everyone is rational and well, so we are always seeking motives. If we try and reason with mental illness, aren't we, by definition, in denial about mental illness? The media looks at "smash-and-grab" robberies in search of a motive, pointlessly trying to reason with something unwell and irrational. Again, we call mass shooters cowards, which is like calling a person having an epileptic seizure "inconsiderate."

There's an ad on the internet, "Grandma Attacked by Coward." It's an ad for a personal alarm called the SafeAlarm. It shows a video of this woman being attacked in a supermarket parking lot, maybe a purse snatching. If the perpetrator is whole, healthy, and well, then perhaps he can be called a coward. But nobody well, healthy, or whole has ever done this. So we must say "ill" before we'd ever say "coward." How we name things matters so much that it could mean the difference between horrible things continuing to happen . . . or not. Bringing folks back into the family delivers what we all long for. The stillness in control, reminding us we are in the same world.

THE BLINDFOLD

KHALIL STOOD UP TO EULOGIZE HIS DAD, WHO HAD BEEN gunned down. His father, Deondre, had worked at Homeboy for some years, though he had many moments when he found himself derailed by addiction and mental torment. He was the 261st person I buried because of gang violence. Toward the end of his life, he'd send me texts with videos of AR-15s and half-consumed bottles of Fireball Cinnamon Whisky, with desperate pleas to buy weapons from him as well as many other hugely unreasonable requests. I kept urging him to go to rehab again. His teenage son spoke of his father with great tenderness and an ache for the time he now won't have with him. But he closed his remarks with this: "My dad was not perfect." He points to all of us. "And he never expected you to be perfect, either." None of us are well, until all of us are.

David Brooks, the *New York Times* columnist, asks the question on a podcast: "Why are we so sad and why are we so mean?" But sadness and meanness aren't the problem. They point to the problem. They remain clues of conditions that need our tender care and attention. We recognize that these clues always point beyond themselves to states we need to address. Merton used to say that we are eternally understood by the God we have. And this God draws us to a more complete understanding of each other.

Brooks goes further in an *Atlantic* article asserting that we have "become a society in which people are no longer trained in how to treat others with kindness and consideration." But cherished people will cherish people, just as surely as the traumatized may likely cause trauma. I'm not sure that one needs to be trained to cherish. In jails, it is now quite common to embrace behavior modification mainly because it will keep the peace and make jailers happy. It will control folks and society feels better as a result. But behavior modification is not about healing. It's about making society feel at ease and comfortable. We say "build character" because we think it may well require a hammer and nails. Behavior changes when people are cherished. It doesn't mean you don't teach things. At Homeboy, we have every manner of therapeutic class and group—anger management, grief and loss, and "Character Matters." But all of our structured resources are secondary to the cherishing culture we nurture into place. You cherish character into flourishing. You don't build it or train for it.

Joseph and I wind down a conversation in my office, and he stands to leave. I've known him since he was a ten-year-old in the projects. His father was a gang member who died of a heroin overdose. Joseph followed suit as a gang member and heroin addict but never succumbed to his own multiple overdoses. He's doing well now and back working at Homeboy Industries. "I think life," he says, "is just removing the blindfold."

I agree with him, but ask, "What do you see, Joseph, when the blindfold falls?"

He pauses, then gently pats his chest. "Goodness." That's right. Unshakable, and nothing can touch it. Our goodness is without dispute. God isn't hoping for our goodness, since we are already good. God longs for us to see it. Indeed, goodness is "the house we never left."

The moment comes when we see God has no need to measure our goodness, since we all are undeniably good. No need to be perfect. The blindfold falls, and we see how unsophisticated it is to believe that "bad people doing bad things" could ever be how God sees. God has less interest in our behavior, since God only longs for us to be joyful. If we seek this joy, behavior follows. It is not about good or evil, but sadness or joy. We realize, for example, that we couldn't really speak of, say, fascism, without speaking of wellness. Or racism, misogyny, homophobia, anti-Semitism, and xenophobia. Anyway, the list is long. These things are descriptors, not identifiers. We know that such illness doesn't touch goodness, though it might, for the moment, touch fitness.

Certainly, Jesus heals blind people. But their wellness is not about sight, really, but seeing as God does. The Hebrew Bible has many examples of humans being shown the vision of God. The starting point is when our Wild God looks at us and says, "You are precious in my eyes, and I love you." We then take that vision and intend to see in each other (and ourselves) our unmistakable, soulful preciousness. We look beyond behavior and see only what God sees. When this blindfold falls, we focus on what is precious in the soul of the person in front of us.

Sergio comments on the guy in the Gospel who pleads with Jesus, "I want to see." Sergio writes: "Wanting helps you climb out of needing."

Kevin pays me a visit. I haven't seen this nineteen-year-old gang member "in a minute." He sits in front of my desk and I try to put my finger on what is different about him. Then I see it. He has a new tattoo, Old English script arching over his right eye. I lean in. "PER-CIPIENCE." Now, I'm an English major, but I've never heard of this word before. Kevin is only too eager and a little too self-satisfied to tell me what it means. He smirks. "It means perceptive, to have a good understanding of things." Pretty good. Perhaps, even, to see as God does. New eyewear.

James Allison says, "Sin is an addiction to being less than ourselves." It still comes down to seeing. We are not willfully strangers to ourselves. Homies are stuck in the cave as a hiding place from a bombardment of hurt.

Visiting a classroom of high school kids, Adrian answered virtually every question with "Life is beautiful. Always keep a smile on your face." Not sure he even noticed that he kept repeating himself. He wasn't "being less" than himself. He just couldn't see who he was through the layers of trauma and abuse that impaired his vision. He, as yet, was unable to absorb the pain of his older brother being gunned down and his father dying in a car accident six months after that. (The Highway Patrol officer called. Adrian answered. The officer asked if his mother was home. When Adrian said no, the officer told him, "Well, today you are a man." And then told him his father was dead.) At thirteen years old, Adrian shut down, and he still thinks he was seeking "money, Benzes, females, and designer clothes" when he joined a gang minutes after his father died. The cave as a hiding place can soon become the sending place. Eventually, Adrian came to see that he was not seeking anything, but fleeing quite a bit. Cherishing coaxed him out of the cave, and the light of day took it from there.

The mystic's eyewear brings into focus the hidden wholeness in everyone. Then our lives become living reminders that we are all made for loving and that the true measure of our love is to love without measure. We don't get saved from ourselves but to ourselves. The blindfold falls and we see our undeniable goodness. Like the rich young man who asks Jesus: How do I get me some of that eternal life? We think salvation means eternal life . . . life beyond this one. But the root of the word "salvation" means whole, well, healthy, sound, and healed. Not about sin but wound. The rich young man is being invited to his own wholeness, to real joy, not a life of deprivation in following Jesus. Jesus says, "Be perfect, as your Heavenly Father is perfect." There as well, "perfect" in Aramaic means "whole." As Khalil alerts us that his father was not "perfect" and neither are we, it is an invitation to wholeness, not to get everything right.

We are all made for loving, and once we help each other to see this, we realize how difficult it becomes to harm anyone. The proximity of rivals to each other at Homeboy forces a realization. Our loving truth helps us to see that we are held in the soulful preciousness of our enemy, the guy we used to shoot at. And this realization grows exquisitely mutual, and that encounter is profoundly sacred. The act of cherishing fashions this meeting of two souls who find their hidden wholeness in their radical sameness.

Jesus invites the tax collector, Levi, to follow, and he does. This inclusion leads to no end of grumbling from folks who think Levi should not be among the invited. The grumblers want to talk about sin. But Jesus wants to talk about sickness and health. This is why He came, He tells us: to effect wholeness. My friend Mary Rakow suggests a more full sense of Jesus arriving to die for our sins. "The invisible is made visible for my sake." The Incarnation helps us catch sight of what our truth is, and it has next to nothing to do with sin. It's what Levi and Joseph glimpse when the blindfold slips. Goodness made visible.

I received a ranting text from a good friend, a therapist. He called the occupant of the White House at the time a racist. I texted him back and said that "racist" was a descriptor and not an identifier. He, like all of us, is unshakably good and belongs to us. I told him that one didn't need to be a psychiatrist to know that the president was not whole. Though, I suspect, one has to be well to know that he isn't. No one wakes up in the morning and says to himself, "You know, today I think I'll try malignant narcissist, with a side order of sociopathy." He didn't choose this illness; it chose him. This illness makes him worthy of our compassion. Unfit to be president, but worthy of our compassion. Racism, anti-Semitism, misogyny, and homophobia are just how his illness presents. He needs help and healing.

My friend texted me right back. I don't think he was happy with my expounding. Hours later, I was sharing my textual conversation with a homie *de confianza*, in my office. I told him that my friend signed off: "By the way, racism is NOT a mental illness." The homie, quizzically, said to me: "Well, what else would it be?"

This was exactly the sentence I had texted back to my friend.

Perhaps the word "illness" trips us up. But we all engage in behavior and responses that are less than whole, balanced, and healthy. God's tender invitation is that we be well. It's not about morality but staying true to our deepest longing to let love live through us. A candidate for president ended his Christmas message on social media: "Merry Christmas. And may all my enemies rot in hell." Now, if my father had sent such a message, all my siblings would gather the next day to hold an intervention for him. We would recognize the broken and wounded spirit such a message points to and try to establish real help. It is how we assist each other to regain our footing and restore our vision.

I suppose one could label racism as evil, but then that would mean we have decided not to make progress. "Evil" stops us dead in our tracks and we are immobilized. Like Jesus thinking the guy having seizures is possessed by a demon. Jesus literally "demonizes" him. Case closed. But if it's epilepsy, then . . . here's a pill. Progress. I call racism horrible, like Camila kicking in our front door. Words matter. Because if it's horrible, you can seek to get underneath the undeniable pain of it all without demonizing, dehumanizing, and othering. Only then can we forge a path to healing and restoration.

"Sin" and "Evil" don't get you to comprehension. After a mass shooting in Nashville, a GOP Tennessee member of Congress said, "We're not gonna fix it . . . Criminals will be criminals." Later he said that Congress can't legislate against sin and evil. Case closed. If it's evil, end of discussion—there's nothing more to do, except, I suppose, shake our fists at bad people who don't belong to us.

In the documentary *The Truth vs. Alex Jones*, a group of Sandy Hook parents sits around a table. One victim's mother speaks of her encounter with a woman on an elevator. The mother wears a pendant with a photo on it and the woman asked her about it. "It's my six-year-old son. He was killed." The woman asked how and the mother answered quietly, "I'm from Sandy Hook."

And the woman responded, "But Sandy Hook isn't real. It didn't happen."

Then the mother emphatically tells those gathered around the table: "The woman was not crazy." Maybe "crazy," like "evil," also trips us up. The Buddhists say, "Ask a different question." No one healthy spreads disinformation. No one well buys it. Can you be whole and think Sandy Hook didn't happen?

The goal is not to save our soul but to spend it. Our authentic discipleship, then, is to grow in love, not goodness. Growth is not about becoming less sinful, but more joyful. I was sitting next to a homie on a plane. David was a terrified first-time flyer. I was enthralled in my book, and he seemed to be increasingly annoyed that I kept reading, especially during some pretty intense turbulence. "Why are you not freaked out by this?" he asked me, louder than he meant to be. I patted him on the arm and resumed reading. After we had something of a screeching, hard landing in Los Angeles (had we not been seatbelted we would have ended up in the laps of the folks in the row ahead of us), he turned to me and deadpanned, "I did not like our driver . . . at all." Like the plane was an Uber. My sense is that God is always rooting for us, longing that we become reservoirs of joy for each other. David and I, to this day, laugh about our "driver." We rest in unconditional positive regard with each other, and it gets us to the "reservoir." We spend our soul doing this.

On a DC trip, Louie Pham never says thank you. Not to the waitress. Not to the cabdriver. Not to the total stranger who gives us directions. He never says thank you. He always bows slightly and says, "I appreciate you." As the youngest inmate at seventeen on a Level 4 yard, he ended up doing twenty-four years. He appreciates things. Before takeoff and after landing, he gets on the phone and speaks Vietnamese to his mom. His tenderness and gentle tone with his mother transcend language. He would always close the conversation in English with "I love you." "Now I don't just exist," he tells me, "I have a life."

We can often be self-congratulatory in our declaration of addressing things head-on. Racism, homelessness, anti-Semitism, poverty, crime . . . again, the list is endless. We don't make progress on anti-Semitism because we stand against it, but rather when we get underneath it. One of the reasons we fail to make progress in taking on these vexing issues is that they are always about something else. If we address what they are truly about, then the by-product of our effort is to see these things dissipate. I learned early on that gang violence was about a lethal absence of hope. "Standing against it" would not have moved the dial. But address the despair, and watch what happens to the violence. It's not about right and wrong but hope and healing.

Edward James Olmos screened his film *American Me* in the gym at Central Juvenile Hall. He invited me there, along with some actors from the film, to help field questions after the screening. The film is somewhat bleak, and I suppose Eddie meant it to be a scared-straight, cautionary tale for these gang members who fill that gym. The film ends, and there is utter silence. Eddie invites comments and questions. Finally, one kid stands and points to the wall where the movie had just been projected. "So, you're telling us . . . there is no hope." And he sits down.

Eddie scrambles to point at the same wall. "No . . . I'm saying there is no hope . . . in this." He points at the blank screen to indicate the lives just depicted. But it was too late. The despair had popped out of the tube and there was no returning it.

The Gospel warns against putting new wine into old wineskins, and it's a good caution. One translation says that if you do this, "your fullness will pull away." A very good caution. Our fullness can get distracted and get pulled away from our center. The frightened, damaged self can take center stage. This happens—only all the time. We need to catch ourselves. How do we help each other keep our fullness from pulling away?

I call Saul into my office. He was cleaning the glass that encases me there. I check in with him. He's an affable guy, always quick with *cariño*, affectionate at every turn. He's eternally grateful for everything, and he expresses his gratitude constantly. You might say this is part of his practice, that it brings *alivio* to him. It allows relief from the weight of things. He's proof that our gratitude and tenderness praxis alters our brain. He comes across as sincere and thoughtful. He's suffered in the usual ways that gang members do. Home life was often a horror show. His humor is pliant and smart. He spent time at Pelican Bay State Prison in Crescent City, the most notorious of California prisons. But he says, "I was stationed in Crescent City." Then he adds, "Makes me sound more like the military."

At the end of our brief check-in, I ask Saul if he's afraid of flying (which he's never done before). He tells me: "I discovered long ago that if you're afraid of dying, you'll be afraid of living." Not bad. I ask him if he wants to join me and another homie on a trip to DC and Boston to give some talks. He is beside himself with "YES" and he's giddy and jiggly in his chair. "Damn, G . . . You're a blessing in the sky." I'll take it.

As he tells his story before large crowds in the nation's capital and in Boston, he becomes increasingly more vulnerable in each telling. He knows how to edit and present his life in a way that is genuine and quite moving. He's proof that our stories save us. Many standing ovations. Hildegard of Bingen, another mystic, writes, "Dare to declare who you are. It is not far from the shores of silence to the boundaries of speech. The path is not long, but the way is deep. You must not only walk there, you must be prepared to leap." Saul declares who he is at every talk, leaping like crazy.

When we fly home, Saul leans into me at one point and whispers, "You know, G, I think I want to learn how to talk fancy."

"'Talk fancy'?" I ask.

"Yeah, you know . . . what's that language they be speaking, where the guy is going to work, and he's out on the sidewalk, and he's waving to his wife and kids up on the porch and he says, 'Ta-Ta.' What's that language he be speaking?"

I think. "Um, English? British?"

Talk fancy. When someone who feels deeply invisible is reminded that their story matters, that there is goodness and nobility inside and it's beyond question, when total strangers applaud your struggle with compassionate admiration—who's not gonna want to talk fancy after that? Saul could ask himself, *What message does my life send?* And now he likes the answer. Soulfully precious. His truth. I suppose this is what it feels like when your fullness is intact and has not been pulled away.

This kind of relational engagement offers folks on the margins a broad-shouldered resilience. It gives a kind of muscular hope, an assurance that a steady, harmonizing love can infiltrate the distance that separates us. Saul doubted that he was worthy of love. But bravely he traversed the terrain of his own vulnerability, moving from his protected, armored heart to a tender one, able to connect with others.

In the middle of a very hot summer, Jairo screenshots me a cartoon of Santa and Rudolph the Red-Nosed Reindeer ice fishing on a frozen lake. Santa is fishing at a good COVID distance from Rudolph, who is experiencing some difficulty. He yells to Santa, "Hey, Santa, my ice hole is frozen." And Santa says, "Language." Jairo texts that this reminds him of me. (Who knows why—it's either my physical resemblance to Santa or the fact that I can often be heard yelling, "Language.") I see him later when he shows up to work at the Homeboy Bakery, and I ask him why he sent me this cartoon in July. He responds, "I don't know. I guess I'm starting to like Christmas now." That's the sound of a damaged kid finding his footing in the ground of his being and falling into oceanic love and acceptance. A muscular hope. Brain altering. Character cherished into being. Wendell Berry writes: "We arrive at the ground of our own feet and learn to be at home there."

A sergeant who oversees the gang unit at the LAPD's Hollenback Community Police Station says that gang violence is thornier to address because it is rooted deeply in the neighborhood history. "The solutions will take time and should include more gang intervention programs in which workers, often with a gang background themselves, help young people make better choices." Behavior change. Modify how they choose. It is the well-intentioned though quintessential outsider view to think the symptom of violence has its roots in "bad choices." What would we need to abandon in order to make progress in reducing gang violence and in police reform? The notion that there are good people and bad people and that we just need to corral folks into better decision-making.

The truth of the matter is this: if you're loving, you're healthy. If you're healthy, you're loving. Furthermore, a healthy person is a holy person. We are all hard-pressed to recall any loving person who wasn't healthy, or a healthy person who wasn't loving. I've seen this with gang members. A great deal of the response to them is about "choice theory." How can we get them to make better choices? But, of course, not all choices are created equal, and not everyone has the same shot at it. Like the NYPD detective, after a terrifying shooting on the subway, suggesting that more cops be added to the subway: "We have to make life more uncomfortable for the bad guy." In the same breath he says, "The guy must have had some grievance." Discomfort is unlikely to enhance anyone's health, nor does it lead to more loving. We all have grievances. No one healthy shoots up a subway train to resolve them.

This idea has long undergirded our opposition to capital punishment. The death penalty has never made us safer. It's only made us lesser. To say nothing of the fact that there are no "bad guys." Only broken people in hopes of gentle notice. It helps us to ask: What happens to our unshakable goodness when it meets up with despair, trauma, and mental illness? Blindfolding happens.

There are eighteen thousand independent law enforcement agencies in the U.S. We have asked them to solve every piece and part of crime: mental illness, domestic violence situations, self-harming folks, homelessness, fentanyl use. They aren't trained, really, to do all this. So we think the answer is to train them. Clearly the police matter, but there is a cost to asking them to do it all.

The headline on HuffPost this morning is "He Hated Black People." It was an article on the tragic shooting deaths of three people in a dollar store in Jacksonville, Florida. Based on the internet breadcrumbs left by the man who did this, the tragedy was deemed a hate crime. His rifle had a swastika emblazoned on it. Deeming it racially motivated actually doesn't help us. It might even keep us from preventing such a horrific thing from happening again. For it will only paralyze us in denunciation, "standing up to hate," all the while preventing us from truly helping the mentally ill, who do not choose this anguish. It keeps us from comprehension, which is God's view. You don't "stand up" to a cough. You treat the lung cancer.

A recent study reports that "80 percent of mass shooters are in crisis." That's inaccurate. Truly, by definition, 100 percent are. What would we think of the other 20 percent? That they are crisis-free? As long as we think that a rational and healthy person could possibly do such a thing, then we can't make progress.

I knew a homie, Milton, who couldn't read at all. He was in his late teens, and his illiteracy caused him great shame. I was honored he would share this embarrassment with me, and I arranged remedial help from tutors. I had a dream about him. He's standing in front of a classroom of his peers. And he's holding the Bible. He says to the class, "Give me a minute." And in silence, he pores over the book of Genesis. Then he closes the book: "Okay, here it goes." And he proceeds to tell the whole story. I told Milton my dream. He understood the depth of hope that was laced in it. He became anchored in his truth enough to want to make progress in his life. To stand confidently in his own skin, like in front of that classroom, freed of shame that had once issued in violence. A heart enlarged to a divine proportion.

When I speak of the reasons why a kid would join a gang, there are three nesting buckets of profiles. The first bucket, the largest sphere that holds all gang members, is despair. The lethal absence of hope. The second smaller bucket is trauma. The wound and brokenness that keeps a kid from transforming pain. The third and smallest bucket is mental illness. Consequently, when homies come to Homeboy Industries, they generally carry one of three burdens: despair, trauma, or mental illness. For homies, there is usually one dominant burden, though it can be fluid, on a continuum of severity. But Sparky has a really hard time imagining tomorrow; Lefty is stymied by the crippling memories of abuse; and Slim occasionally hears voices.

I run into Gato in the parking lot and I ask how he's doing. "Same drama, different day, but I'm struggling and making progress. I got my beams on." What do the high beams reveal? Hope in darkness, an ability to be with anguish, coming to terms with what was done to you and what you did in your brokenness. Progress looks like bowing

to life's sorrows and betrayals. Freed of shame, there is a robust accep-
tance of what is. Gato's being opens to the shared pain of the world.
All of this happens when you "got your beams on."

In the old days, when I would roll up on my beach cruiser to some
brawl or other in a part of the projects and see some older *vato* from
back in the day kicking it there, having returned to his old stomping
ground, I would become my least "Gandhi." I'd make a beeline to
him and question his presence. The older *vato* would counter, "Gee,
imagine how worser things would be if I *wasn't* here." We all need to
cleanse our delusional narratives.

I would then ask him, "Who is still out here gangbanging?" I'd
tell him: "The very young. The very weak. The easily punked. The
mentally ill. Which one are you?" Looking back, I can see how this
approach of mine reflected more my ongoing frustration with the
levels of violence rather than a true contour of cherishing. A real con-
fidence in cherishing is hard-won and not once and for all.

Most incidents at Homeboy Industries happen when someone lets
another "take him to that place." The set-tripping, provocative insult
that questions your manhood, your courage, and your whole being.
In debriefs with the fighting factions, one of the senior homies will
often say, "You let him take you to that place," or "If you stay ready,
you don't gotta get ready." Fabian, a wisdom figure and now the direc-
tor of the Homeboy Art Academy, in his early days as a senior staff in
our headquarters, bumped into an old rival who unleashed a firehose
of invective in Fabian's general direction. Fabian didn't argue with the
torrent. He calmly went outside to have a cigarette. A younger homie
who witnessed all this was both perplexed and admiring of Fabian.
He followed him outside. He asked Fabian why he didn't volley back.
"'Cuz I know I'm gonna go home tonight and my lady will call me

Babe"—and he takes a long drag on his cigarette—"and my kids will call me Dad." A pure narrative.

I was giving a retreat in the Midwest. In one of my talks, I had been often quoting the words of God to Jesus through the clouds: "You are my Beloved in whom I am wonderfully pleased." I've always liked that translation. It was brought to me fifty years ago when I was a novice, directed on an eight-day retreat by the great Peter Fleming. I've never forgotten his version. "In whom I'm wonderfully pleased."

One of the retreatants comes to see me. He is married with three young kids. As the homies would say: "He's stressed out da game." He struggles to navigate his marriage, job, and parenting. He's finding it all overwhelming. He is out on a walk through a field and when he returns to the road, he discovers that he has all these "stickers"—burs that have glued themselves to his sweater. So, he turns it into a mantra exercise. "I decided with each sticker I pulled out, I'd repeat that line you said this morning, from God to Jesus . . . like they were words meant for me." He mimes for me, excising the burs, "'You are my Beloved, . . . I think you are perfect.'"

I stop him. I tell him the line is "In whom I'm wonderfully pleased." He seems surprised at this. Then I suddenly feel a great rush of emotion. "Wait—that's what you say to your kids, don't you, when they feel frustrated, overwhelmed, and less than. When they are beating themselves up for the lost game or the failed exam. You hold them, you look them in the eye, and you say, 'I think you are perfect.'"

He nods, and we both feel the fullness of it, while our tear-filled eyes say as much. Jim Finley tells us that we have this notion that God is in heaven and that God is in you. Then he proposes, "What if God's heaven is you." Perfect.

We can wander into knowing deeply that God is infinitely in love with us. Once we are quickened and awake to this, we know that holiness is God's will. God's pleasure is expressed to Jesus not after a long marathon of his ministry, but at the very beginning, as he is baptized and sets off. The pleasure of God, utterly reliable, is not connected in any way to a performance well done. Like Jesus, and the guy pulling out the burs, we know that God's pleasure is in us and who we are. I spend my days telling gang members that they could not be one bit better. I've never felt a moment when that was anything but true.

Ask the homies what they watch on TV, and more often than not, they'll say the Food Network. My guess is that after being forced to concoct "spreads" and other contrived delicacies in a prison cell, they find *Diners, Drive-ins and Dives*, more than a little intriguing. They like *Chopped*. There's something about that basket. "Here's what's in your basket." We all connect to that. Zen master Bernie Glassman paid me a visit at Homeboy before he died. He couldn't speak and was in a wheelchair, but his wife and caregiver carried on while Bernie's still-soulful eyes sought connection and found it. I'd met him years before at his Greyston Bakery in Yonkers. I brought homies to marvel at it and to galvanize their imagination. Bernie writes of the Zen cook who creates a five-course meal using only the ingredients in front of him. Here's what's in your basket. The emphasis here is that we have everything we need.

Paco seemed to have a litany prepared of all the things for which he needed money. He's young but already has small kids. Predictably, he was a wreck when he asked for funds. He thought he had to win me over. "I have to buy food, I got my phone bill, gotta buy toilet paper to wipe ourselves."

I looked at him. "Paco," I asked, "did you think I needed a fuller explanation for the use of toilet paper?"

"Oh yeah . . . right."

We laughed. I wrote a check, gave it to him, and we hugged each other. He asked for a blessing. Before he reached the door, he turned around. "You know, G . . . you have savoir faire."

"Say what now?"

"You have savoir faire." Each time he said this, he shifted his entire body in sort of a French way.

"Where'd ya get that from?"

"Some guy said it about you. Yeah, 'Father Greg's got . . . savoir faire.'" Again, with this odd French contortion.

"Do you know what it means?" I asked.

"Nope," he said.

"Neither do I." And we hugged each other again—you know, as the French would. Opening the basket and seeing that we have everything we need for a solidly good meal.

Because goodness remains intact for everybody, there is no need to judge anyone. But we are always making health assessments. For example, I fly on a small Delta plane from Knoxville to Atlanta. I have to board my flight to Los Angeles, but we all need to wait in the air bridge for our luggage. Nothing arrives. Finally, a gentleman shows up, quite apologetic. "There's a glitch," he says. They can't unlock the door to get our luggage from the plane. Everyone is calm and kind and even appreciative. No one is grumbling or barking or unraveling. We all have flights to catch, connections to make. I suppose I'm grumbling to myself, "*Pinche* Delta," but everyone else is Zen, relaxed, and still quite grateful to this poor guy who keeps returning to update us on their progress. (They are making none.) It wasn't that we lucked out and got VERY good, decent people on this flight. We didn't get people with "character." We got healthy people. Except for the guy muttering, "*Pinche* Delta" to himself, these folks were near whole and well that day. There was a serene balance and an evenness. Goodness and character had nothing to do with it.

Asa Hutchinson dropped out of the race for the 2024 Republican presidential nomination. A former governor with a qualified résumé, in an earlier era he would have been a contender. Times are different now. Then came a decidedly snarky and condescending response from the Democratic National Committee: "This news comes as a shock to those of us who could've sworn he already dropped out." The White House, and the president himself, swiftly issued an apology to Hutchinson for the mean-spirited takedown, which Hutchinson appreciated. "It meant a lot to me." It wasn't that the young staffer at the DNC was mean, but young and not yet whole. And the adult in the room who suspended his race, and the one who apologized, are healthy people.

At Homeboy, it's not about pathology; it's about wellness. Not mental illness, but brain health. It's not about cognitive behavioral change (the nagging cough). It's about a culture that cherishes (addressing the lung cancer underneath the cough). Those of us privileged to work at Homeboy don't give the homies "the reason to live"; we cherish them until they can find their own. We don't supply them with a purpose, but, rather, nurture a culture where they can discover one for themselves. A child tries to see her preciousness reflected in the eyes of her parents. But if the parents don't give this focused attention back, the child can't see it. We try to make up for lost time. As Theresa, one of our singular therapists, often says, "It's never too late to have a happy childhood." Homies are decidedly embraced at Homeboy, and as the African proverb goes: "The child not embraced by the village will burn it down to feel its warmth." We say, "It takes a village," which means "All hands on deck." But it needs a village, an actual community where folks are embraced. It needs villagers.

Over dinner in a New York restaurant, Demetri tells me and Frankie how, some years before, he was shot multiple times outside a car wash. He's on the ground bleeding out. He manages to pull out his cell and call his mom. She only had a landline. "She's always home," he says. "The phone rings and rings. . . . My mom has a bad habit of unplugging the phone so she can plug in the vacuum. I'm bleeding to death and she's vacuuming." This harrowing moment gets rendered hilarious in his telling of it.

On this trip, besides endless sightseeing and catching the musical *Wicked*, we drove to Connecticut to give a talk. Our presentation took place in a gorgeous modern chapel with amazing mosaics lining the walls, packed with college students, faculty, and community members. Demetri stood up first and told his story. He got to a juncture of his account where he felt the most desperate in his life. "I mean, I just got out of prison, no job, I was shot, problems at home, homies putting pressure on me . . . I didn't know what to do. I mean . . . FUUUUUCCCCKKK." The entire chapel sucked in huge gulps of air. Then Demetri realized that he'd just said "fuck" in this hallowed place. His shocked realization gave everyone the permission to move from gasping to laughing. When he continued his talk, he said of Homeboy, "They highlight you there."

A couple years later, Demetri drank himself to death. He would show up drunk at the office, heedless of our urgings for him to let us take him to rehab. I visited him toward the end at the hospital. I hardly recognized him, tubes everywhere, but he had a shock of hair. Typically, he'd shave himself bald, revealing his tattoos. I said, "Damn, dawg, I didn't recognize you. You got hair."

He could barely speak, what with the tubes, but managd to say, "No choice." We smiled at each other. Then his eyes flooded with tears. "I shoulda listened to you, G." He cried a bit. I anointed him. As I left, he said, "Tell everyone at Homeboy, I LOVE HOMEBOY INDUSTRIES." He died the next day.

Still, we find our roots that are eternal and cannot be tugged out. Resurrection has to be embraced with every breath, and it changes how we see things. All of us are saved; there really is no alternative. The only difference is being aware that this has happened in you. Knowing it is everything. We feel "highlighted." Even in a final moment that wants to "tell everyone at Homeboy."

The essential paradox of Jesus is: you lose, you gain; you die, you'll live. Letting the blindfold fall allows for so much. At a talk in a crammed assembly hall at Red Cloud Reservation, nineteen-year-old Chino bravely addresses students and faculty, nearly all Native Americans. "Now I don't look for trouble. I look for positivity." He has tattooed on his forehead "Tough Love." He put it there as a counter to "Fuck Love." He has a different take on "Tough Love"; he means it as resilience, a fierce love that barrels through, hangs in there, and holds out for something enduring. "I hold out for *cariño*, to be embraced again." And he said of his parents, abusive alcoholics, "How did they expect me to be a different person, when they didn't show me different?" Finally, he says: "I don't want people anymore to fear me. I want them to love me." All human longing is contained in wanting to be embraced. The warmth of the village. Hold out for *cariño*. Then our love is tough and fierce, able to embrace others.

During the Q and A at a church talk I give, a little kid sitting in the front row, maybe a second grader, waves his arm wildly and hoots, "OOH, OOH." He wants my attention. They race a microphone to him and he stands, taking his time to formulate the question that he's desperate to ask me. "Has anything bad ever happened to you?"

There is a great echoing of laughter. When it subsides, I say, "Never."

Next, a grim and stern woman poses a question. "What happens, then, to the bad guy hanging on the other side of Jesus on the cross?" I told her that Jesus doesn't think he's a bad guy. Jesus comprehends. "This day. With me. Paradise." It's a promise good for both *ladrones*.

Sergio emailed me about a pastor who sent out a notice about a film on Jesus that was going to be shown: "Please invite someone who is unsaved." It helps to remind ourselves that for the first five centuries, Christians believed that we would all be saved. Someone asked me who will be saved? I told him, "Everyone is going to heaven, but God hopes you know that heaven is also here and now. He doesn't say, 'Ya wanna go to heaven, then do this.' He says, "Do this . . . heaven." Feed the hungry, welcome the stranger, visit the guy in prison. Heaven. Do this . . . It's where the joy is. We can live in the forever now. It helps us say "never" when asked if anything bad has ever happened to us.

Our passionate heart truly never ages; it is always living in the forever. It is pure presence and grounded in belonging. "At the ground of our own feet." It places us outside of nothing. Our within-ness is central, and we fully engage, participate, and reveal that separation is illusory. You are anchored in the arriving day. Before poet Mary Oliver died at eighty-three, she concluded that she had learned these three things in her living: 1) Pay attention. 2) Be astonished. 3) Share your astonishment.

Many years ago Spider and Mongo pay me a visit in our storefront office on First Street. They are sixteen years old and "into" their gang and just got released from the Hollenbeck police station. Spider is the wily and more clever of the two. Mongo is a big ol' lovable lug. He adores Spider and would follow him into any old mischief at all. They were playing hooky from Roosevelt High and were kicking it at Hollenbeck Park. They are blazing it and see a police car coming in their direction, so Mongo tosses the baggie of chronic into some bushes. They proclaim all manner of innocence to the cops, who rummage through the bushes.

Then one of them asks, reading the baggie he has found, "Which of you is José Gomez?" Mongo—José Gomez—has put a strip of masking tape across the baggie.

"And on it," Spider reports, "he wrote 'Property of José Gomez.'" Spider looks at Mongo, who is now giggling, "*Serio pedo . . .* Who does that?" As we laugh, we acknowledge our astonishment at being grounded in belonging to each other. Separation doesn't exist, and we are nestled in this magnificent within-ness. I'm sharing my astonishment with you.

The imprints of trauma can keep you from inhabiting the present moment. The meaning of the word "trauma," in its Greek origin, is "wound." Our wounds can taint and spoil an appreciation for the present moment. Homies walk into our headquarters with a trauma that is preverbal, for the most part. They are followed by the tyranny of their past. And yet, the Incarnation means right here, right now, in this body, time, and place. God, with flesh and bones.

Chuy asks me once, "Do your siblings ever visit you?" I tell him yes. "Do they admire you?"

The question gives me a start. I say, "They admire YOU."

Then he tells me this: "I always saw myself as a *desmadroso*, you know, always ruining everything." His trauma has begun to move from the preverbal to an inkling of finally inhabiting the next healthy thing to do in the present moment.

His stepfather repeatedly beat down his mother. Chuy helplessly witnessed this as a constant in his childhood. Finally, at a family gathering, when he was seven, where great drinking was taking place, Chuy confided in one of his visiting uncles about the violent abuse of their sister, Chuy's mom. Later that night, four uncles arrived at Chuy's house and knocked on the door. This seven-year-old boy, sleeping in the living room, woke up and let them in, then they went to the kitchen, beat down the stepfather, and stabbed him to death. He witnessed the whole thing. "Yeah," he tells me, "I'm a *desmadroso* . . . I ruin everything."

For Zen Buddhists, a vow is not a promise to do something and then you feel bad if you don't pull it off; rather, a vow is a stance and an intention. For Chuy, his vow and intention, since arriving at Homeboy, became not an obliteration of the memory of this trauma but letting go of his attachment to it. He could now intend to inhabit the healthier stance, brought back to loving in the present moment. He could even finally love this seven-year-old who opened the door that night. My admiration is total.

One hopes to create a safe place where we can let our pain visit. We open the door and let it in. We welcome it. We allow it to teach us. We hold the pain until it transforms us. Still, we don't let it overstay its welcome. "Dare to declare who you are." The blindfold falls and we see what we've always been meant to see: the light in our soul. Meister Eckhart tells us that "God is no farther off than the door of your own heart." We realize this divine essence and acknowledge that this light is in us all. Perfect. We are God's heaven. Not a potential for goodness, but without dispute and undeniably present now. We want only to have an unbroken awareness of this light in everything and in everyone. The door of our heart. We want to see. Truly, a blessing in the sky.

A TRIBE TO END
ALL TRIBALISM

THE HOMIES HAVE A STOREHOUSE OF PRISON SAYINGS. THEY ALL seem to know them and yank them out whenever necessary. If a homie agrees with another, he might say of him, "He's on point like Stacey Adams." Another one addresses regrets. "If 'if' were a fifth . . . we'd all be drunk." This one deals with a lament over one's past. If only I didn't get in that car. If only I didn't follow her home. If only I passed on smoking that sherm. Everyone can get stuck in yesterday and in regret. We move forward in love because it seems to be the only thing that can conjure up tomorrow. It helps us imagine a village that transcends tribe.

There are two parades the day Jesus enters Jerusalem. There is Pilate and his show of military power and force, heading to Jerusalem from the west. Then there's Jesus, on a small donkey humbly entering the city from the east. Jesus' trek and mission displays a way of life whose hallmarks are inclusion, nonviolence, unconditional loving-kindness, and compassionate acceptance. The parade of warhorses announces the threat of violent force, coercion, and the oppression of the poor. The "triumphant" entrance of Jesus is not an indictment, but an invitation. Village transcending tribe. Jesus doesn't draw lines. He erases them.

Of course, people can point to the turning over of tables. Jesus, at this juncture, seems full of indictment. Lots of ink has been spilled on Jesus infuriated at the merchants in the temple, upending tables, and fashioning a whip to make his point. Another prison saying: Jesus was "hotter 'n fish grease." This event, without question, enflames and encourages those who wish to kill him. But perhaps there is something more muted happening here.

A member of the Homeboy board is Michael Tubbs. He was the first African American mayor of Stockton and the youngest mayor ever of a large city in the United States. He is a foremost proponent (with Pope Francis) of the universal basic income (UBI). He says, "We need to upset the setup." That's what we're invited to do by Jesus in this moment. It is not a free pass to "be taken to that place" of unbridled rage that ends up only being about "me" and creates the inevitable "them," the reviled "other." It is more subtle when we upset the setup. It creates kinship.

I gave some basic instructions before Adrian and Jamal spoke to one thousand people gathered in a DC ballroom. "You have seven minutes to tell your story. What happened to you, getting into your neighborhood, incarceration, hearing about Homeboy, and what you have found there." I also added these two concrete tips. "Don't begin by asking, 'How y'all doin'?' Your audience is at a loss to answer that. And don't tell them how nervous you are. It makes the people worry about you." Jamal was first with his seven minutes. It would disparage deer to say he was in the headlights. His talk was seven seconds. In that space of time, however, he managed to ask, "How y'all doin'?" and he fanned himself while announcing, "Damn, I'm nervous." Adrian used his full seven minutes.

In the drive back to our hotel, before I could say anything, from the back seat, Adrian patted Jamal on the arm. "You did good, my boy."

Jamal was disbelieving. "I felt like I blacked out."

Adrian reassured him, "I'm tellin' ya, you did good." Adrian pulled the favor right out of Jamal and he was left feeling favorable. All lines erased. "I know I'll be better next time." So, what's the usual "setup" here? Kick folks while they're down, mock, and "talk masa"? Find the vulnerability and cheaply exploit it for an equally inexpensive laugh? Adrian upset the setup, and its issuance was a tender kinship. This beats turning over tables.

Martin Luther King's last book was called *Where Do We Go from Here: Chaos or Community?* We find our way out of chaos and its dispiriting tribalism by standing against forgetting that we belong to each other. At Homeboy Industries, rival gang members who used to shoot at each other trade hostility for a cherishing lens that just hopes to see as God does. It creates a tribe of cherished belonging that wants to end tribalism itself. It has no interest in forming yet another tribe among many. It longs to be yeast that will produce whole loaves. It's the sourdough starter that points the way to a new way. Indeed, the front porch of the house everyone wants to live in. A refusal to make villains of anybody. Community, not chaos.

Freud thought that "Love your enemies" was unrealistic. Yet Jesus was dedicated to reality. Everything shifts when we decide to look at enemies and only wish well-being for them. And when we cease to see them as enemies at all. Our decision to be a well-wisher is born of our having been cherished in this same way. And it is this nurturing that keeps ifs from becoming a "fifth." But who can wish well-being for enemies? A mystic? A holy person? No. Only folks moving toward healing and health. Charles Pickering says that "a healthy democracy requires a decent society" where people are "honorable, tolerant, generous, and respectful." But who can pull that off? Only a healed person can do that.

I'm on a Zoom at 6:30 a.m. with a classroom of inmates in an Illinois state prison. All of them had just read my book *Tattoos on the Heart*. Every single one of these "students" will die in prison. An inmate stands and addresses me at one point: "Even though all of us have 'all day' . . . life without . . . we don't throw in the towel. We use the towel to bind wounds. We tie all the towels together. Then we throw the whole thing over the wall. We try as best we can to be helpful in the world." Yeast. Creating whole loaves. Healed.

The homies can sometimes cross the line when they are bagging on each other. Joel is famous at this. You can see the quickness of his repartee and you know it is headed straight into that wall. He is quite famous around here for going too far. He is bantering with a somewhat volatile homegirl, Maya, who is holding her own. They are in the tattoo clinic in our third headquarters some twenty years ago. Not sure what he says exactly, but Maya becomes enraged and chases him out of the room where the doctor is removing someone's tattoo. She is not playing. As Maya pursues Joel through the building, she grabs a serrated knife perched in the drying tray in our small kitchen and chases Joel down the hallway, screaming and waving the *filero*. Joel runs into Cara's office and slips under her desk. Cara is in the middle of a meeting.

When Maya reaches the glass door to Cara's office, Moreno, standing nearby, calmly and quite adroitly slips himself in front of the door. Maya stops. Moreno, a much beloved older homie, who would be gunned down a handful of years later, blocks Maya's entrance. He doesn't scream at her, nor blanket her with shame. He quietly affirms her rage. "Yeah, Joel can sometimes make ya want ta kill him." This modulates Maya's breathing to a slower register. "But," Moreno continues, "Joel loves you and you love him. So . . . you don't wanna kill him." Maya slowly hands the knife to Moreno. He hadn't even asked her for it. He hugs her. Tie the towels together. Throw the whole thing over the wall. Bind the wounds.

It's not for nuthin' that the one who enters that locked room after the Crucifixion and says, "Peace," was the one bearing wounds. He carries them. He doesn't move beyond them; he moves with them in the room. Not merely tolerating but, indeed, embracing them. He makes friends with the wounds. We don't move on from trauma but learn to move with it. His remarkable presence announces some exquisite comprehension and room for every foible, failure, and shame. We are held in these wounds.

We had thirty minutes until we would land in Pittsburgh. Traveling with me this time were Pablo and Alvaro. We were enjoying the extra legroom of the bulkhead exit row. Alvaro, in the middle seat, leans into me and says, "I need to use the restroom." I point to the one nearest our row. "No, I'm gonna go back there," Alvaro says, pointing to the back of the plane. While he's gone, there is a strange sound, a chirping. I fly a lot. I've never heard this sound before. Alvaro slides back into his chair, out of breath. Is it me, or does our entire row suddenly smell like skunk? In a flash, an irate flight attendant is standing directly in front of Alvaro. "Is this you?" she shouts, holding her cell phone inches from his face. On the screen is his name from the passenger list. A suddenly nervous Alvaro nods up and down. She's gone as fast as she arrived.

"What happened?" I ask him.

"Nu-thing," he responds, which is, of course, what one says.

I head to the back of the plane, and I find this flight attendant, still shaken, talking to a colleague. "Excuse me, he's traveling with me . . ."

"HE IS?" she barks.

"Did something happen?"

"YES. We think he was smoking in the bathroom."

"Um . . . what happens now?"

"I don't know. It's the captain's call." None of this was communicated in a pleasant tone.

I return to my seat, and I am less than pleased myself. I resort to the silent treatment, of which I am not proud, but we're about to land anyway. When we step off the plane, there are two suited men and seven uniformed officers awaiting Alvaro. They whisk him away, always in sight of us, and stop not far out of the gate area, where two officers question him. We can't hear anything, but I can see Alvaro gesturing wildly, feigning a kind of *I'm new to your country and your ways.* Pablo turns to me during this, puts his arm around me, and tries to console me. "You do know he's retarded."

"I do now," I tell him.

He was smoking a "stizzy," a vape version of marijuana.

Like the guy bearing all the wounds and saying, "Peace," nothing disqualifies us from inclusion. "Peace" acknowledges how we are all afraid, locked in a room after the Crucifixion or igniting a chirping sound in the restroom at the back of a plane. Welcome is always being extended. "Ours is not a caravan of despair," Rumi writes. We sometimes want to exclude the folks who, from their damaged place, color outside our lines. We lament so much. "If 'if' . . . were a fifth." But this caravan of ours is spacious and wide. It helps us move forward in love and conjure up tomorrow. Even when we issue a silent treatment as a way to draw lines, they are always being dissipated by the guy bearing wounds and whispering, "Peace."

I was speaking to a friend who has dedicated her life to minister to the unhoused. "People don't become homeless because they run out of money," she told me. "They become homeless because they run out of relationships." This assertion has resonance with gang members as well. There is an Irish saying: "It is in the shelter of each other that people live." At Homeboy, we've come to believe that we enhance belonging by seeing to it that no one runs out of relationship.

Gera relapsed. It had been a couple years since meth had that kind of hold on him. He was in a vise grip for four days. He had been working in the bakery, and folks there knew he had slipped. Their urging was clear and straightforward: Just come in. So, he did, shrunken in shame. He came by my office a couple days after, just asking for a blessing. He's a short, very stocky fellow, and this morning he had on a hairnet and a Homeboy Bakery apron, which was dusted with flour and faint smears of chocolate. When I ended the blessing with the sign of the cross, he looked up at me, tearful, and said, "When I came back to the bakery, they didn't say 'Where WERE you at?'" Now he was sobbing and struggled to speak. "They all said . . . all of them . . . 'We're glad you're back.'"

Isaac, a case manager and homie, gave me an explanation of his job: "We don't box trainees in. We surround them with love." We are always giving each other access to a muscular hope, born of everyone doing their part. Surrounded with love. Real shelter looks like this.

I met Rulis, a wonderful man, when he was a munchkin in Pico Gardens housing projects nearly forty years ago. His mom, Lupe, was a legend of leadership and vision in the community. Hers was one of the most massive funerals over which I've ever presided. Rulis is in charge of onboarding new trainees at Homeboy as they begin their eighteen months with us. He told me, "The most difficult moment in the intake process is the question "Who is your emergency contact?" He told me the homies are undone and flummoxed by the question. Like the woman who touches the hem of Jesus' garment, there is power in connecting, the force of relational wholeness. We are all just trying not to run out of "emergency contact people." And we see that all longing and human desire is just love trying to happen. Folks then get to fall into the immensity of their surprisingly reliable goodness. We find ourselves surrounded and awakened to this in community.

I engage in something of a meme ministry. The practice of texting is a way, I think, to communicate microaffirmations. Our hope is always to zero in on the precious soulfulness that God honors in each person and wants us to recognize. James Loder calls it "non-possessive delight in the particularity of the other." I want to text homies out of the blue and tell them how proud I am of them. It can calm the chaos.

I get so many texts from gang members that, rather than type so many words in response, I sometimes let crazy memes do the talkin'. Once I had to have a huge melanoma excised from my shoulder. (FINALLY, the chip that folks have wanted to knock off got removed.) The surgeon removed all the cancer. I had clean margins. I was telling people that I had "secure borders," then I realized that refers to Mexico, not melanoma. Thousands of homies hear about it and are all well-wishing. In the interest of brevity, I send a playful meme to all of them, with assurances that I'm fine: it's a brief video of Mr. Bean in scrubs, pulling down his mask and giving an enthusiastic two-thumbs-up to the patient, indicating a successful operation. I sent one to a homie named Jerry who was concerned about my health. He writes back, earnestly, "To be honest with you, Pops . . . your doctor looks creepy."

I nearly burst my stitches. The fact that he thought Dr. Bean had performed surgery on me was all I needed to feel connected in relational wholeness to him and have "non-possessive delight" in the "particularity" of this wonderful kid, Jerry. We keep relationships afloat however we can, playful, joyous, and sturdy. Always choosing to be well-wishers, "microaffirmers." It is how tribes break through to real cherishing communities beyond the insular confines of their narrow definition. As Pope Francis calls us "toward an ever wider WE."

A new trainee on his first day, Alex, sits in my office accompanied by a Navigator, who asks him, "What do your homies call you?"

"Lazy," he says.

"Well," the Navigator tells him, "from now on you will be called 'hardworking.'"

The next day, a very confident Alex plops himself down in a chair in my office. "Can I ask you, Pops, how old are you?"

"Guess."

"Mid-seventies?"

"You're fired."

"But, Pops, I just started yesterday!"

Alex was a very tiny guy and his lady would hide him in a stroller and wheel him into the house so her parents wouldn't know he was spending the night. Before long, he was able to secure Section 8 housing, so he and his lady and child could live on their own. When his second baby arrived, he sent me a pic of his newborn in an orange onesie and pretended the message came directly from the baby: "I just spent nine months inside. Can you get me a job? I can even be a Navigator. I'm pretty sure I'm gonna test clean."

Alex's father was a heroin addict. When he was a child, his father would rouse Alex in the middle of the night and leave him in the car while he would try to find tags to peel off cars or hop into backyards and steal dogs and marijuana plants. Alex was supposed to honk discreetly if someone was coming.

Alex told me that "the turmoil was terrifying" as he grew up and later when he was gangbanging. He told me that whenever he saw violence, "I was always running to it. It was suicidal." When he encountered the usual stressors of life, he said once to me, "It was easier in prison . . . and how can that be possible?" Homeboy is hurt introduced to connection. The hem of the garment. Later, Alex was able to say: "Homeboy softened me and I don't mind even saying it. This is my heart zone—coming here." It's the difference between understanding Alex and believing in him. He could assess his time with Homeboy this way: "I see you seeing me." And then he moves on. As Stevie puts it, "stability before mobility." As he says goodbye on his last day, I tell Alex, "You're the best."

He waits a beat. "I'm starting to believe it." This is when, as Hafiz says, God begins to lose "God's shyness in the world." This newly discovered, extroverted God lavishing us with the certain truth of our own goodness. Altogether reliable.

Before I was to give a big address at Valparaiso University in Indiana, they had a panel on reentry. On the stage were eight former inmates. It was a very diverse group: Black, Latino, Asian, and a couple white guys with long ZZ Top beards. These eight men shared about their life in prison, and one spoke of their common experience. "All of you," he said, pointing at the audience, "need to know each other in order to understand each other. But we," he continued, referring to the men onstage, "none of us know each other, but we understand each other." At the time, I thought it was pretty wise and said so, in my talk that night. But later I thought that what transcends even understanding each other is believing in each other. If we only join those who have the identical experience we do, it creates a tribe of the like-minded and permits disqualification from the "wider we," the village of our shared humanity. Together, we can throw the towels over the wall, all hands on deck. All villagers are invited. No need for anyone to absent themselves. Beyond understanding is believing. We can all do that.

Jeong is one of Korea's most defining cultural concepts. It is a deep connection and emotional bond. Much like mitzvah, it's an engagement of righteous action that is endlessly connecting us to each other. It creates lasting kinship and encourages generosity. It's forever, and different from love. It fosters mutual understanding beyond the tight circle of those who share your experience. People feel seen. It's like *ubuntu* in South Africa. It posits that our health as a community is inextricably linked to the thriving of everyone in the community. What gets cultivated is a warmth and kindness that genuinely wants another to be happy. It enables us to shift people to say, as Heather McGhee writes, "We've found the enemy and it's not each other." Alex is starting to believe he's "the best." But his health (and holiness) is not once and for all, but presents itself sporadically. If we can foster a "heart zone" more reliably, we can make it all less episodic.

In an earlier chapter, I mentioned Saul ("blessing in the sky"). On the Boston leg of our trip, we arrive and it's quite freezing. Saul and the other homie, Brandon, select a car at Hertz. Saul hops into the back seat and immediately says, "Hey, G, the car comes with a back scratcher," holding up a huge ice scraper with a large brush.

The next morning I want to send the two of them off to see the sights while I answer thousands of emails. I call Saul, who is in his hotel room, and I ask what he needs to do to get ready to "get lost" in the city. "I just need to have my coffee, then get an oil change [take his 'morning masa'], then take a *playa* [shower] . . . and I'm good to go."

At dinner, he told Brandon and me the following story. Saul stands alone in front of some old courthouse; Brandon is off somewhere. Saul takes a selfie. In front of him, in a small corner park, are two homeless men sitting on a bench. One of the guys sees Saul and yells, "HEY, DON'T TAKE MY PICTURE!"

The calmer guy next to him says, "Relax, he's taking a selfie."

"I DON'T CARE WHAT HE'S DOING . . . YA JUST CAN'T BE TAKIN' PICTURES OF PEOPLE."

Saul, instead of making a beeline in any other direction, walks across the short, narrow street, toward the hostility. As he stands there, the quieter of the two says, "Don't mind us, we're crazy."

Saul looks at them and sees them. "That's okay. I'm crazy, too." He extends his hand and tells them his name. They do the same. The quiet one is Louie. The ranter is Sam. They talk for a while until Saul tells them he has to go. Sam has now become the quiet one. "Hey, Saul. I've lived in Boston all my life. Do ya need directions or sumthin'?" Saul had softened them into some tender corner. He had erased lines that had been drawn pretty clearly. There is a kind of dosing that goes where relationships haven't yet been and ensures that no one runs out of them. From chaos to community. One dose at a time. Our extroverted God, no longer shy. And asking for directions softens us all.

We had some eighty uniformed community engagement officers from the Los Angeles Police Department filling our reception area. It put all the homies on edge. The police were there to get a "training" from some select homies, who would seek to "soften them into a tender corner" when it came to their view of gang members. Before they were to head up to our conference room for the presentation, they were all milling around with the greatest of discomfort. It was an odd sight to see them line the whole area and assiduously avoid contact, eye or otherwise, with the gang members waiting for services. Homies shift in chairs, giving the officers the hairy eyeball. Two tribes staring each other down.

Then homie Rafa stands and points at an officer. Rafa has been with us a very short time and completed a decade behind bars. The officer walks warily toward him. Everyone recalibrates their focus and shifts all attention to the cop and the *cholo* now walking up to each other. A bristling tension is in the air as an unaccustomed stillness rests in the lobby. Everyone recognizes that the two are seeing each other.

They get face-to-face and each speaks the other's name. Then they embrace and hold their hug for a really long time. When they release, both men are crying. It had been twenty-five years since they were best pals in elementary school. When things stay separate and isolated, they stiffen into survival mode. The hairy eyeball. We all can embrace a narrative that sometimes reenforces the separate tribe. We live in the shelter of each other.

I spot Little Hector sitting in the lobby of Homeboy. We all call him "Little Hector" to distinguish him from Big Hector Verdugo, who helps run the place, and because Little Hector is very small. He is stocky and covered with tattoos, head to toe. He's just chilling in our reception area, looking as serene as any monk would. He no longer works here. Our job developers located good employment for him beyond Homeboy, so I'm thinking maybe he lost the job. I go to him.

When he sees me, he leaps up and throws his arms around me. "What are you doin' here?" I ask him.

"It's my day off," he says, grinning broadly. "It's just . . . I know everybody here. I feel comfortable right here. Plus, it doesn't cost me any money."

The Irish say, "You are the place I stand when my feet are sore." Who we are, truly, is loving attention, and our practice keeps reminding us of that truth. Our practice is to open the mind, quiet the heart, and it doesn't cost nuthin'. You return for a dose when your feet are sore.

They asked Thomas Merton, "What do the monks do all day?" He answered: "Fall down. Get up. Fall down. Get up." This perfectly describes Homeboy Industries as well. At Homeboy, we foster a community that practices friendship, where love comes first, since that's where the power is. And love promotes well-being. It wants what God wants: wholeness for everyone. It keeps us honoring the dignity and nobility in each person. Otherwise, we find ourselves stuck and can become the vending machine that says, "No longer accepts change." We train the mind to tenderness and cherishing. A fresh revolution. You fall down, we'll help you up.

Omar needed stuff for his new apartment, like a refrigerator and furniture. I told him to send screenshots from Amazon of what he needed. "Don't hold back."

He texts: "I wasn't planning to." Then he sends me a pic of a king-size bed frame, costing nearly seven thousand dollars. I text him:

"PLEASE hold back." The Buddhist notion of joy is *mudita*, having a joyful heart. Julian of Norwich thought joy was the true human fulfillment. Mysticism is limitless belonging. We enter into the fullness of God, and we go from feeling ourselves, as they say, "a drop of water entering the ocean," or Omar, trying to get a seven-thousand-dollar bed out of me . . . "The ocean entering a drop of water." Omar can say, "I belong to the whole, becoming whole." We are constantly being offered joy instead of judgment. Joy helps our patience ripen into humility, and then we all become a healing presence in a wounded and wounding world. Chaos is tamed and community is formed. All in service of a "wider we."

Sometimes we lionize our anger as holy, akin to that righteous rage in which the prophets engaged. Brian McLaren writes, "I love . . . therefore I get angry." I think: Not so fast. The problem with our anger is that, by definition, it makes everything about ME. It can't be. Plus, our anger (again, by definition) has to have a target, a THEM. There is no way around it. Even if our rage is directed toward "racism," it still involves people, so it is still saddled with a THEM. Our anger begins with a dislodging . . . "These are the folks who don't belong to us." Precisely because it separates, we know God doesn't share in our fury. Fury sets up tribes and draws lines. God never sees things this way. This doesn't mean there isn't work to do. There is. The role of the prophet has been, of course, judgment, but also hope. We would do well to name the things that contradict the purposes of God. Again, not just to point things out, but to point the way. Oddly gang members at Homeboy have always taught me how to visualize the avoidance of separate camps. Homeboy is not the answer, but we think we might know what the question is: What if we believed that we belong to each other? Upset the setup.

My friend Pádraig Ó Tuama speaks of the "troubles" in Northern Ireland as "belonging gone wrong." The same could be said of American gangs, of our partisanship, and of the tribal nature of all the camps so dominant in the country at the moment. Real belonging should dismantle aloneness and caress into being a radical humility and a dedication to loving-kindness. Belonging should exhibit the bravery of our own curiosity. Curiosity conquers our fear more than bravery will. In fact, curiosity IS bravery. This very curiosity conquers our fear of each other and ushers in a welcoming spirit. My brother Jesuit Christian Verghese says, "Fear indicates a lack of relationship." This welcoming spirit dispels fear. Then we are able to love our neighbor, not just as we love ourselves (we actually don't do this so well), but as we love our child. Belonging gone right.

In truth, we don't really "love" our children. We cherish them. Cherishing is love fully engaged. Cherishing is tenderness in action. Like everyone at Homeboy, Miguel, our head of security, is a constant hugger. His hugs, though, come with a side order of vigilant "pat-downs." Then he will open his immense jacket, for he is an imposing *vato*, and indicate an inside pocket. "Do me a favor, put that thing in this pocket and come see me after you talk to G." Upon the guy's return, Miguel will walk him down the block, return the weapon, and say, "Now, don't ever bring that here again. Respect. Always." Love can't pull that off. Only cherishing can. Cherishing is love with its sleeves rolled up and its coat wide-open.

Gloria spoke plainly. "My mom was love. My dad was rage." Then her mom, her protector, died of cancer when Gloria was ten. No one now stood between Gloria and the outsized abuse of her father. The physical violence directed at her was unrelenting. When she spoke to her father and even remotely complained of his treatment of her, he'd say simply, "Grow some skin." She was lodged, for a time, in an idola-trous belief that she was all that was wrong with her. Shame was what needled her, "until I found Homeboy, and it gave me a blood transfu-sion." Previously, her conclusion at watching her life unfold was that "it's only gonna get worse." Gangbanging, drug use, and prison filled every gap in her world. Finally, she was able to say, "Homeboy is not my tribe. Homeboy became my village."

Gloria stared into the very abyss of the catastrophe of her life and gradually became aware of the range of the plasticity of her mind. She had survived it all and was cherished into imagining a new way of being. A community of belonging stared down her dislocation until she found her capacity to reinvent. It enabled her to become a mother to the kids who had been taken from her. She found generativity, and, yes, she grew skin, the resilience born of loving attention from the entire village.

The sidewalk preacher would say to Anthony, "Jesus loves you."

And Anthony would look at the guy and say, "How so? 'Cuz that fool don't live here." He could later say that he found life in the proj-ects always punishing. "The pain never stopped." He went through a very tough period when he was simply too wounded to be rational. When his own father was not in prison or beating his mom or selling and/or slamming heroin, he'd manage to look at his young boy, An-thony, and say, "*Venga, mi rey.*" Anthony would much later reflect on this. "He gave me that crown." Many years after that, Anthony came through Homeboy and found his flourishing joy. Crown regained. Once I watched him from across the street talking to Luis, a gang member, now homeless and always high on meth. We spoke after-ward of this encounter. "I tried to give him his crown," he said. "I told him, 'It's just fallen off. You can put it back on again.'"

We were literally minutes from this tiny fundraiser we were holding in the back of a restaurant. Danny, one of our bakers from the earliest years, was sitting at a table in an adjacent room, trying to put some finishing touches on his speech. I would walk past, and he would be thinking out loud: "Homeboy is one of the best . . . um . . . Homeboy is one of the best . . ." He would tap his pen to his lips as he searched for the right word.

I leaned in. "Endeavors?"

He glowered at me. "Uh, not a word I would use."

Just trying to be helpful. Isaiah writes, "Do not turn your back on your own." "Own" referred to blood ties. You would kiss these kin on the lips. Then the early Christians upset the setup. They would kiss each other, expanding the notion of "our own." Planting big wet ones, in the most inclusive way, is the "endeavor" of the village.

There's a minor altercation in the reception area. Ghost is in the front row, waiting to see me. Two rows back sits his homie, Sal, also waiting his turn. Ghost has been drinking a lot. It's midday. He's eighteen and was recently thrown out of the house. Lucky walks by all the seated folks and says something provocative to Ghost, and we're off to the races. Security steps in and separates everyone. Ghost, in his drunkenness, is directed outside. I follow from my office as he is being escorted down the block. I hand him my card and say, "Come back when you're sober, son."

I call Sal in next, and he sits in front of my desk. Before we can get down to business, I see one of our senior staff, Rulis, walk by. I flag him in and have him take a seat on one of the chairs that line the wall. I know Rulis has seen the whole burgeoning conflict. "*Oye*," I ask him, "did Sal get involved in that little *pedo* right now with Ghost and Lucky?" Rulis assures me that Sal was an innocent bystander. I tell Rulis to stay while I dispatch Sal. He's a famous *pediche*, and I know he's going to make some monetary request, so this shouldn't take long. "What's up, son?"

"I need some help," he says. I reach into my pocket and peel off two twenty-dollar bills and, from under my desk, fold them into a discreet wad and go to shake Sal's hand. He waves me off. "I don't need money," he says with some emphasis.

Now I turn to Rulis. "He doesn't need money. So now I'm going to ask him, 'What is it that you DO need?' and he's gonna say something like, 'I need a brand-new transmission.' And I'm gonna say, 'Um . . . a new transmission requires money, right?'"

Now I turn back to Sal, who has commenced great chuckling. "*Mijito de mi cora*, what do you need?"

When Sal can rein in his giggles, he says, "A brand-new transmission." (Really. I had no idea. I just pulled transmission right out of my . . . hat.) I hand him the wadded forty bucks and say, "Poof. Begone." We hope against hope that in the familiarity and giggling comfort, the wounded will be radicalized and transformed forever in God's sustaining mercy. Emergency contact.

Lefty walked right past me. I was leaning on this half-wall partition, telling Norma, my assistant, that I was heading out to give a luncheon talk. Lefty didn't pat me on the back to acknowledge his presence. It would have deterred him, and alerted me. People later would say they saw him walk past me. This was twenty years ago, before we ever thought to recruit the homies to be security guards.

It was never possible to have Lefty work at Homeboy. Initially he was too young, then he was too deeply involved in his "barrio," unwilling to step away from it. When he was twelve, he infamously set off a cherry bomb in our restroom. Clearly, he was the culprit. Too many eyewitnesses. Though, when I spoke to him after, he tearfully insisted, "I DIDN'T DID IT!!" At fourteen, he went to Juvenile Hall for the first time. From the dayroom, he yells, "HEY! I NEED TO TAKE A SHIT."

The probation staff member in the office, something of a linebacker, slowly pushes away from his desk and enters the dayroom, where Lefty sits on a bench. He mad dogs him: "What did you just say?"

Lefty, in an instant, inhabits his actual age, "I need to go poo-poo."

Homies call it "running amok." This was Lefty, a tiny little guy, relentlessly gangbanging. I found him one evening in the projects, clearly packing a gun. Someone had given me an impressive small and polished arrowhead. I put it in his hand and explained what a talisman was. "Keep it in your pocket. Whenever you think you might do something crazy, grab it, hold on to it, and remember this moment." His eyes were wide and respectful. He nodded. A very sweet kid who listened when you asked this of him.

Lefty was eighteen when he whizzed past me that afternoon, determined not to make me aware he had entered our headquarters. I left to give the luncheon talk.

Rushing through our narrow hallway, through the kitchen, past the conference room, and out the back door, Lefty was determined to get to Youngster, who was in the alley. Youngster was the same age as Lefty, with a very similar and horrific, trauma-filled childhood, propelling them both to "run amok." Lefty and Youngster were enemies. In my special birthday calendar that I've had for forty years, on Youngster's birthday, it says simply "Youngster." Next to it, in parentheses, it has this identifier: "(who makes me laugh)." This is how I distinguished him from all the other "Youngsters" I knew. He was so smart and quick, and his sense of humor was way beyond his years.

When a kid is this funny, I think maybe he'd test genius if he ever went to school.

Lefty crossed our parking lot and shot Youngster many times in the chest. He then quickly escaped down the alleyway. Several homies and homegirls saw it all from the parking lot. They witnessed Youngster fall and bleed out before the ambulance arrived.

The ambulance took a while to show up. A small group of Homeboy staff surrounded his body. Someone retrieved a clean towel from the kitchen and gently placed it where the bleeding was extensive. One of the folks there was Monxi, a job developer at Homeboy. He had a manila folder with some letters in it. He held it over Youngster's face on this hot summer afternoon. He didn't fan him but held it steady there. As the sun moved, so did Monxi's protective shade. Even after it was clear to all that Youngster's spirit had left, still the manila folder kept vigil over his face. A sustaining protection and comfort in the passage. And a towel for the binding of wounds. This is what villagers do.

I told you that whole story just so that I could get to the singular nobility of Monxi holding that manila folder, blocking the sun for this kid who made me laugh.

Lefty still sits in prison all these twenty years later. Not for one moment has any of us seen him as outside "our own." I saw "Tribe Called Human" written on a wall in New York City. The village is the place of the great belonging, where the "tribe called human" can be enhanced and furthered. It is the place of what Luis Rodriguez calls "shared well-being." Loving human beings build loving societies, resting on a web of mutuality. A world where every world fits, the Zapatistas say. The diversity of our tribes is our superpower and not cause to lose hope. The presence of so many gangs at Homeboy Industries doesn't slow down our belonging but heightens the harmony of the whole. We find our harmonious strength there and choose willingly to be each other's emergency contact person. Becoming well-wishers erases all lines. It is what occupies us in the "heart zone" as we move forward in love, conjuring up tomorrow.

5

ACATAMIENTO

ADRIAN STANDS IN FRONT OF AN ALMOST ENTIRELY WHITE group of criminal justice majors and graduate counselors at Loras College in Dubuque. He's a stocky guy, with the expected tattoos etched on his neck and face and shaved-smooth head. After fifteen years in prison and only a brief three months with us at Homeboy, his trip here was his first in a plane and the only time he's stood in front of a group to tell his story.

Actually, he had been out of state before. During his tenure locked up, they transferred Adrian to Oklahoma from Calipatria State Prison. It took them thirty-nine hours on a bus. He was shackled at the ankles, the waist, and the wrists. The inmates never got off the bus the entire time. "To me," he tells me, "it was torture."

The most noticeable feature of Adrian's presentation is his sweet-natured voice. It's not just younger than his thirty-four years. It has a quality that is so pure and gentle. It is soulful and true. You just want to listen to him. His authenticity keeps folks spellbound.

"I know that most people would take one look at me . . . I mean, you would see me walking down the street, and you would cross to the other side. But what you don't know about me is that if I only had one dollar left and you needed it, it would be yours. If you were shirtless, I'd give you mine. If your car conked out, I'd help push it." Everyone in the room believed him.

On February 27, 1544, Saint Ignatius of Loyola, the founder of the Jesuits, writes this one word in his spiritual journal. He proceeds to use it a lot for the remaining twelve years of his life. Before he dies, he goes back and circles the word wherever it appears. Now, I know Spanish, but I had never heard this word before. *Acatamiento*. It comes from a somewhat archaic word, *acatar*, which means to look at something with attention. It seems to have been used when the king gives a servant marching orders and the servant is delighted to convey, "I'm happily on it, Your Majesty."

Acatamiento gets translated as "affectionate awe." Certainly, this word and meaning was singularly born of a mystical connection between Ignatius and the God of love. It seems to have found its genesis in a contemplation of the Holy Trinity. For Ignatius, the Trinity was revelatory of God as relationship itself. But this awe is not how we stare lovingly at the Trinity, because the Trinity has zero interest in our doing that. For Ignatius, the Trinity was a notion of God to be imitated. It urges us to shape our lives around relationship with others, but particularly with awe and affection to those cut off. It's meant to be our stance at the margins. Relationship itself. It is directed to those whose belonging has been severed. The folks we cross the street to avoid. It is how we greet people who carry so much. It can inaugurate a fresh movement if we abide in it.

When Ninja went to prison, his daughter was only two years old. His bond with her was already sure and deeply affectionate. She would run to him and brighten whenever he entered a room. Every moment he could, he spent with her, deepening their connection. Then he got locked up. Quickly, he was put in the SHU (Security Housing Unit, or solitary confinement) for excessive fighting, and it was two years later that he got his hands on a cell phone and FaceTimed with his wife. She brought his daughter into view, and he asked his shy girl all manner of questions. When the conversation seemed to have run its course, his now four-year-old daughter walked out of the shot, but he heard her ask her mother: "Mom, who's your friend?"

One's reaction to this moment could be "Well, you shouldn't have gone to prison." Or, "Why do you keep getting into fights and sent to the box?" Or we find a stance more willing to hold the pain of it, even with affectionate awe, that permits suffering to be a teacher for us all. Oscar Romero tells us, "There are many things that can only be seen through eyes that have cried." Clearly, "good" or "bad" is not how we should frame anything. I think we still are surprised that God does not do this. *Acatamiento.*

Ignatius combined the best of the medieval mystical tradition with Renaissance humanist ideals. He embodied an affective piety that connected so fully to the humanity of Christ, always insisting that we move from our singular, isolated mystical moment (love is God's religion) to an enduring mystical consciousness (loving is how we practice it). Through it all, affectionate awe deepens into loving humility. It is a heightened awareness, becoming more like

Christ. Enfolded in a Christ consciousness. We experience it all in union with Jesus. Held with loving humility. Now everything is holy.

Over fifty years ago, there was an older gentleman, Ray Keefe, who was a year ahead of me in the Jesuit Novitiate. He was too old to be ordained, so he entered as a Brother. He had been a traveling sales-man during the fifties and sixties, and whenever he found himself in a strange hotel in a strange city, he'd put himself to sleep by perusing the local phone book in the town. It was kind of a litany of saints. He'd trace his finger down the page of names and collect odd ones. He had a million of them. Here are two I remember: "Fardy Lardy Dover" and "Phuckey Mae Bailey." He would hold these people in prayer and even found the holy in the wacky ones. Besides being an odd pastime in the pre-internet era, he always saw it as some way to affectionately connect to the place where he found himself located and to its inhabitants. He held them, and *cariño* was brought to each name. He knew that each human (and odd) appellation was "just try-ing to suffer a little less," as Thich Nhat Hanh writes. He saw the prac-tice as an affectionate consciousness.

To look with attention. The ancient Greek word for attention is *prosoche*. Even the original Stoic notion of *prosoche* was meant to en-hance our progress. It beckons us to an awareness of where we are and who we are with and what is present right in front of us. It jostles us a bit from the narratives we cling to. For if we cling to them, we can't make progress and we won't recognize progress when it's made. Like abandoning the "tough on crime" narrative of the nineties and replac-ing it with a "smart on crime" narrative. I suppose, in part, it's what Jesus meant when he called us to become like a child in our seeing. We are meant to accept the kinship of God as a small child would, with a childlike sincerity and attention. It is authentic. Like Adrian's voice, soulful and true.

At Homeboy, the ongoing invitation is to integrate all trauma and to become less detached and dissociated from it. Still, we are aware at Homeboy that trauma is stored differently from regular, ordinary memory. Homies have learned to survive by living in a habitual dissociative state, a dark cave. Cherishing is the antidote that helps integrate traumatic memories that permits less dissociating. Cherishing interrupts the trajectory of a deregulating, unraveling homie. A trainee points out, "After twenty-three years locked up, I left prison with insight, but I didn't find healing until I came here. And just the insight alone, without healing, deepened my despair." In a cherishing culture, like Homeboy's, the goal is not to eliminate all triggers (which is not even possible), but to create a holding place that equips people to withstand triggers and to integrate them. The traumatized recover in relationship. It's the difference between a lightbulb going off over your head and standing in a room flooded with light. Cherishing coaxes folks out of the cave and into that luminous room.

Nico was just five when his parents were fist fighting in the living room. His father clearly had the upper hand. His mom would fall to the floor, and Nico's father would kick her. What runs through the mind of a five-year-old witnessing this? Nico leaped into action and tried to pull his dad away from the beatings, only to be flung himself to the floor with each intervention. Finally, the father was more annoyed with his interfering son than with his wife and bounded into the kitchen, where an unattended *olla* of beans had been boiling for some time. He quickly grabbed two potholders, hoisted the pot from the flames, and dumped the contents on top of his five-year-old boy. "All my skin came off. Just peeled right off my body. Both my parents told me to don't say nuthin' at the hospital." His dad told him, "In this family, there are no snitches."

When he was twelve, Nico was sent out to sell drugs for his father, to make pickups and collect money. The one time he got caught, he spent some months in Juvenile Hall. When released, he announced his "retirement" from the drug business to his father. His dad was not pleased. "He walked me to the door and threw me out. I never went back. I was thirteen." Looking back on that time, he marveled, "I learned how to sell drugs before I learned how to ride a bike." And he asked himself, "Why didn't I speak up? 'Cuz I didn't have a voice." He came to this conclusion in his own healing at Homeboy: "Actually, I'm grateful to my father. He taught me how not to be one. I appreciate him for that . . . with my own sons." Trauma is the disconnection from the authentic self, and healing in a safe place is the reconnection. We inhabit the depth of this longing to reconnect and, through it all, love is just trying to happen.

Johnny keeps insisting that we have lunch. I don't really do lunch. It takes me away from the office for too long. But I agree to take a quick trip to Yang Chow, "home of the world-famous Slippery Shrimp." We get out of the car, and I tell him, "Thanks for noticing that I've lost thirty pounds."

He surveys me. "Huh. I didn't know hair weighed that much."

I try to remember when we met. He tells me it was almost twenty-five years earlier. He got out of the Youth Authority after having done ten years, a sentence of juvenile life, and heard that his brother, Julio, was living with his lady and their small baby in the back house, over the garage at my Jesuit community. There was a complete apartment there, with kitchen and bathroom. The day after Johnny's release, he came to the main house looking for them, and I guess I answered the door. He recalls this vividly, but as for me, not so much. "We stood talking for a while," he says dreamily. The memory seems to fill him as the recollection does me as well. Then he says, finally, in a confessional tone, "I had tooken a taxi to get there."

I say, "Oh," not thinking much of it.

Johnny wants to complete the thought. "No, I mean literally . . . I took a taxi . . . I jacked a cab . . . to get to you." One still wants to look at everything with attention and affection and not be derailed by behavior, maybe just some awe at how we "stood talking for a while." What gets thrown at us in life can be deemed either awesome or awful. A consciousness filled with *cariño* helps us choose awesome.

A question that often comes up in the Q and A when homies are present is "What would you tell teachers to do, based on what you experienced in your early education?" One homie, Ricky, simply recounted a striking memory. "In the third grade, the teacher would write a paragraph on the board, and our assignment was to copy it. I tried as hard as I could, but before I could finish copying, she would erase it. Always. No matter how hard I tried. Always. It made me feel slow and stupid. And then I felt shame and embarrassment. After that, all I knew was rage that only got worse, and finally I just dropped out of school." He then let that settle a bit, a third-grade dropout. Then he added with great emotion, "Teachers . . . don't erase the paragraph so soon."

We were considered by the mayor of Los Angeles an essential organization during the pandemic. We were never closed for very long. One of the trainees, a single father of a severely autistic nine-year-old daughter, was always late or missing. When I questioned him, he said, "My daughter goes to school, and lately she does this fake cough thing. Won't stop. And in these COVID times, they don't want her at school." I just try and imagine this and can't recall carrying anything as vexing. You start to see this steady, harmonizing love that infiltrates the distance that separates us. You start to realize that God just wants us to be whole, and so we try to restore wholeness in each other. Christ consciousness. Suddenly, you are this autistic child and the father who cares for her.

As we stand in affectionate awe of what folks have to carry, it has the potential to ignite a movement, an insurrection of kindness. The Zen master says, "When we bow, we give ourselves up." I try to remember this whenever I meet with someone. I consciously and slightly bow my head as a reminder to forget myself on purpose. This allows the other to take center stage and brings them into the holding place of belonging. This is how we nurture relational wholeness at every turn. To look at something with attention. We engage in a contagion of kindness. All that's required is attention because it brings us back to the present moment where the bowing happens.

I show up to officiate Ricardo and Katherine's wedding at the Christ Cathedral in Orange County. It had been, famously, Robert Schuller's Crystal Cathedral, until the Diocese bought it. Ricardo was a kid I knew from the projects, and I hadn't seen him in thirty years. I was honored to do his wedding. I was (per usual) unable to attend the rehearsal the night before. (Of course, I always think, just practice walking in and out, you don't need me for that.) Katherine is Vietnamese and she gets up to do the first reading in her native tongue. She reverently approaches the altar, her maid of honor behind her, making sure that her lengthy train does not get . . . derailed. They both bow, respectfully, before the altar. Then Katherine does the reading. When she's finished, she and her maid of honor once again return to the altar, bow, and go to their seats.

There is a song, then it's Ricardo's turn to do the second reading in Spanish. He seems startled when I signal for him to get a move on. I'm just reading along and following the program, which I'm seeing for the first time. He awakens, leaps forward in a few long strides straight to the ambo, and does his reading in serviceable Spanish. He's relieved when he's through, so he makes a return to his seat, when suddenly he remembers and stops dead in the middle of the spacious sanctuary. He's facing the congregation. You can see the wheels turning. His face says, "Wait . . . in rehearsal, I bowed. Yeah, I think I'm s'posed to bow." And then he does. Ricardo takes the whole congregation into his gaze and then does a full-body bow, in THEIR direction. The audience explodes in laughter. Ricardo startles for a second time, reconnoiters, remembers, and turns to the altar and bows, whereupon the congregation bursts into applause. Red-faced, he returns to his seat.

It's my turn to read the Gospel and preach a homily. I come from the "if you can't fix it, feature it" school of presiding. I tell the congregation that Ricardo got it right the first time, in bowing to them. He gave himself up on purpose, with a reverence for the complexity of all that the people in this crowd have to carry. His very esteem and regard placed the folks seated at center stage and indeed created a holding place of belonging. I lead the congregation in applause for Ricardo one more time.

Our practice is about quieting the mind and opening the heart. In doing so, we train our minds to tenderness and cherishing. Giovanni's sister was murdered. She visits him in a dream, some months later. "I'm free," she tells him. "Now live your life free." We recognize that "living free" is to cherish, that this is who we are. Loving attention. We learn "the tender gravity of kindness." Giovanni, in his extraordinary pain, is able to say, finally, "Kinship love is like a trophy that ya earn by learning the way of Homeboy." This recognition keeps us honoring the dignity and nobility in each person, as an ongoing invitation to freedom. Giovanni was able to gush with great emotion, "The last are first here!" How ya not gonna bow?

I was a second-year novice in 1974 when Richard Nixon resigned the presidency. Some thirty of us would cram into the TV room and watch the Watergate hearings every day that summer. We were on top of every turn and development, and we knew all the players from John Dean to Senator Sam Ervin. Our director of novices, Leo Rock, was in the front row every evening to get the Walter Cronkite recap of each gripping day. Leo was not shy in his critique of the Nixon presidency and would contribute something of a punctuated commentary during Uncle Walter's "And that's the way it is" evening summary of the day's drama. On the morning of August 8, we knew the announcement was coming and there was standing room only in the TV room. Leo occupied the middle seat in the front row, right in front of the television. Nixon gave his brief resignation announcement, and cheers were released in the room. I was at an angle a few rows behind Leo, and my eyes were on him. He wasn't jubilant. He stared straight ahead, then I watched him wipe a tear before taking his leave. It seemed that all he could see was wound and damage, and it moved him. I asked him later about his reaction and, given his hypercritical stance with regard to this occupant of the White House, I told him I was surprised by his response. He told me that, in an instant, all he saw was a broken man, and that was his point of connection. To become wholesome, we need living connection with the whole. *Acatamiento* looks like this. We welcome our wound, and it keeps us from despising the other. Connective tissue.

Homies rarely feel that they belong in the world. They have, in a particular way, large territories of fear in their hearts and can be ill at ease. Two homies in Chicago ask a stranger not "Where is Navy Pier?" but rather "Where can we go where we will fit in?" Often, I take homies and homegirls to Niagara Falls before arriving for talks at the great Chautauqua Institution. I'm standing with David and Isaac in front of our hotel at the Falls, pointing in different directions, showing them where they can explore before we go to dinner. "You can go over there, or you can walk up that road."

Then David asks, looking distressed, "They won't mind?" The residents of Niagara Falls won't "mind" the presence of two Los Angeles gang members witnessing this wonder of the world?

I pay the bill for dinner at a Denver restaurant with homies Jesús and Ashley. As we're leaving the restaurant, our waiter sees us and says, "Thank you for coming."

Ashley turns to him with a smile and some emphasis: "No, thank YOU for having us." It was as if we were company in this waiter's house, not paying customers. But "welcome" is unexpected for folks on the margins. They're surprised by it. You fully expect people to cross the street. Like the Samaritan woman at the well with Jesus, we all thirst to belong and find welcome.

A homie whose two sons are autistic discovered early on that they were always trying to signal to him, "Welcome to our world." It took him a while, but he learned to abandon his insistence that his sons become something other than autistic. Welcome. Enrique Flores, whose son is autistic, told me that the Maori word for "autism" means "in one's own time and space." Homies feel like strangers in somebody else's home. Seeing the welcome mat in front of those who are on the margins leads us to a loving humility that jettisons insistence entirely.

It calls us to listen and to truly see the other. Respect for one's own time and space. The book of Sirach speaks of humility and kindness and then says: "Water quenches a flaming fire." The flames that distance us from each other are humbly reduced so we can see as God does. God sees preciousness. So can we.

I've been at this a long time. Homies give me more credit than I deserve in remembering faces or folks who were detained in some place where I celebrated mass long ago. A homie, sitting for some time in the reception area, finally gets called by Julissa to come in to see me. I really don't recall him at all, but I keep that to myself. His name is Martin and he remembers me. He was finally released from prison after a quarter of a century. He begins to cry and says, "Thank you for keeping your word to me so many years ago." I can't recall what word I uttered nor kept to him, but I only want to be as reverent as I can be as we both find some dignified honor in this precious beholding.

At a retreat with Navigators, all homies and homegirls who have come up through the program and are now senior staff each share a difficult moment we had to negotiate. I mentioned that many years earlier, after we had experienced our second murder of our second member of our Graffiti Removal team in less than three months, I sat each member of the crew down and individually polled them: Should we continue or discontinue this social enterprise? Every single one answered a resounding "yes" to continue. All the Navigators present, hearing me relate this, clearly admired the courage and raw bravery of these crew members who wanted the Graffiti Removal team to continue. As I observed their admiration of the crew, my eyes welled up with tears. Twenty years later, I could see why I decided to shut the crew down anyway, even after their expressed determination to continue. I realized now, two decades later, that they all said yes because they saw themselves . . . as disposable. Given all that they have been asked to carry through their lifetimes, they did not deem themselves worthy of eliminating risk. They were all expendable. I recognize now that's why I said no.

As often as I can, I try to pull into our program the sons and daughters of folks who work at Homeboy so that these kids can witness their parents, with whom there can be great estrangement, as working adults. Personally, it was life-changing for me as a teenager to load trucks at the same milk distribution company where my father worked. It illuminated my relationship with him to observe his interactions with coworkers.

I pulled in a little homie, the son of one of our senior staff, to "prize" him a little. I ended our conversation by saying, "I will never get tired of calling you my grandson."

He said to me: "You sure? Everyone gets tired of me." The Buddhists say, "Whatever we resist, persists." If we resist believing that God thinks we're perfect, we fall back into thinking we're tiresome.

Tara Brach talks about RAIN: Recognize what's happening; Allow it to be; Investigate with curiosity; Nurture it and offer tenderness to it. This is easy to say as an acronym. Way harder to actually pull off. It is a worthy and sensible goal nonetheless. Mabel and Efrain have been together for ten years. Not exactly a conflict-free ten years. They are the Honeymooners, except Mabel is Ralph Kramden. *The Bickersons* might be another name for this particular marital TV sitcom. Efrain has a stroke and loses his consciousness for a time. When he comes to in the hospital, Mabel looks him in the eye and asks, "Do you remember who I am?"

He nods and with some difficulty says, "Yes."

And Mabel says, "Fuck." Fardy Lardy Dover.

Still, nothing keeps us from recognition, allowing stuff to be, and choosing a nurturing curiosity through it all.

We are endlessly waiting for people. Paul writes in Corinthians that we should "wait for one another." It's like waiting to eat until everyone is seated at their place. I wish I knew how to accelerate healing and make folks return to themselves with more speed. But our whole being at Homeboy declares, "You know where you can find us." Homies who surrender to the quest of well-being can sometimes be impatient with those who aren't ready to tend to their wounds. I urge Edgar to tell his gang member brother to come in. "Tell him we'll help. We'll start him right away."

Edgar is done trying to drag him in. "Come on, G, he's a grown-ass man." And for emphasis, he adds, "He's got hair on his butthole. He BEEN grown already." But Edgar had many the hiccup himself at Homeboy. After many starts and stops with us, he could finally say, "I left Homeboy all those times before because it was a lot of love to handle around here." He finds a place of stillness and says, "I can handle it now."

A homie was texting me for the umpteenth time, complaining about his coworkers in a warehouse where he often calls them "haters," "stupid," "evil," and "worthless." I responded simply: "People are wonderful." This bothered him greatly. "No definitely NOT, Fr. G . . . what about Charles Manson or Ted Bundy or Jack the Ripper?" I wrote back and said that they were all unshakably good, but too deeply and profoundly ill to be able to see it. I used the example from the day before of the woman who threw her two young kids over the 405 freeway overpass because she was too freaked out by the eclipse. I don't think he was buying it. We mistakenly think that crime is something criminals do, but that's false. Crime is something born of despair, trauma, and mental illness. Addressing these things in people is what affectionate awe looks like in practice.

I would walk the yard, "doing laps" with inmates, as chaplain at Folsom State Prison. The guards hated this. On my last scheduled day as chaplain, I was finally told by the lieutenant to never do it again. I happily obliged, knowing it was my final day. Once, I was "taking a lap" with Puppet on the A yard when an old, gray-haired inmate was coming in the opposite direction. He saw me, and his head bobbed up and down. "East LA," he said, much the same as Cheech would say it. I nodded in his direction.

I turned to Puppet, "Do I know that guy?"

"Best not to," Puppet said. "That's Angelo Buono . . . the Hillside Strangler." Puppet told me that this guy was his first cellie, until he asked for a change. "I always slept with one eye open." I saw Angelo many times after that. He always said, "East LA," whenever we passed each other. He died in prison some seven years later, and I'm glad he was there. But his presence in the world begs the question: What would we have addressed with compassion when he was young and in need of healing that would have changed things? I am confident that more awe would have altered matters.

Beto had a puppy pit bull. He spoke of the dog as tender and gentle and loving to Beto's kids. Someone stole the dog and sometime later Beto found him in a park. "Long story short, let's just say, I got the dog back." I didn't ask any questions. "But the dog was changed. He was aggressive, and clearly he had been tortured. Finally, the dog could no longer be around the kids and we had to be put him to sleep." Living in a wounded and wounding world changes things.

The homegirl Inez shared at a morning meeting that "what I

found at Homeboy was beyond my wildest dreams. Before Homeboy, I didn't sleep, let alone dream. And when I did sleep, I had nightmares." The homies find their power in acting from the fullness of love in them. A great deal can delay that fullness. We learn so much from "eyes that have cried."

The truth about "post-traumatic" is that it isn't ever really "post-." We have to find a way to move with it, as the wounded Jesus shows us. Perhaps Jesus was able to find some curiosity around what he suffered so he could allow it to be his teacher. Allen just took off on one of our in-house lawyers. He screamed at her with the foulest of *palabrotas* and reduced her to tears. She was assisting him in a very thorny child custody case and she delivered bad news—to him, an unacceptable impasse. When he had calmed down long enough for me to ask him about it, he assured me that blowing up was, in fact, a measure of how much he loved his daughters. We were then able to gently explore how the outburst had indicated more work he needed to do.

"Post-" can sometimes suggest "over," but in community, we aren't sidelined by behavior—we are eager to understand what it means. Through it all, the affection does not wane.

I officiate a backyard wedding for Tudy. He works at Homeboy and only invited some thirty-five people. He sets up a nice tent behind the house and several rows of white plastic chairs. Tudy is chain-smoking and taking occasional swigs from a Modelo before getting hitched. When the ceremony is over, I signal a thumbs-up to the DJ to play some song to get the couple out of the tent. It's an informal affair. The DJ yells out, "What song?"

There's silence, until a homie yells back, "'Nowhere to Run.'" The tent nearly blows over from the laughter.

An old man walks up to me after the wedding. "I'm Tudy's father." I shake his hand and tell him how happy I am to meet him. He says, "I understand that Tudy calls you Pops."

I downplay it. "Well, everyone there calls me Pops."

He looks steadily at me. "You've been a better father to him than I ever was." It was heartbreaking. The last thing in the world I would have ever wanted was for this man to feel in any way diminished. But he carried himself as one who had long ago transformed his pain and had learned to live by love alone.

Over thirty years ago, when gang members were constantly running up to cars and competing in the sale of crack cocaine, the customers who would walk up to them on foot were often homeless. When these folks had no money, they'd offer themselves as human punching bags for sport and in lieu of payment, homies would just pummel them. Occasionally, I'd walk into these scenes and interrupt them, or bump into a "customer" with his face rearranged. I would often confront one of the "older heads," and the response was nearly always the same. "Come on, G. He's just a basehead." Disposable. Wounding and wounded.

The gang members who are gathered across the street from the church are out of control. I am overseeing the afternoon wake of one their homies inside the church and have to make regular visits outside to quiet down the raucous gang members posted up near our parking lot. I have known these guys for many years. On one of my forays outside, a homie named Speedy has written the name of his gang with a spray can on a side wall of the church. This is a breach beyond anything I've ever seen. Meth, alcohol, and PCP were calling shots that afternoon.

A very drunken Leo managed to paint over the egregious violation.

He is insistent with me: "I've changed, G." Leo tells me this because he thinks I'd never acknowledge this.

Maybe he *has* changed. But he hasn't healed. He's never been to Homeboy, though I've known him for forty years. He still calls shots for his gang, even as he holds down a job and tries to be a husband and father. He has never known the experience of healing in a community. Not sure the wounds can close otherwise.

Many years ago, five homies return to work after lunch. It turns out they had a liquid lunch. They're all quite staggering and *pedo*. Hector Verdugo calmly tells four of them that they are suspended for five days. Each of the four are deeply repentant and all hoping against hope to hold on to their jobs after the suspension. We keep trying to model discipline rather than "discipline" folks. Beyond imposition is a tender "modeling."

David is another story. When Hector locates him, he is barely standing in the small garden by himself in front of our back curriculum building. He's a very large guy, chiseled, and his fully "sleeved out" tattooed arms are revealed by the muscle shirt he's wearing. He's in high belligerent mode and is not having any of it. Hector tells him that he, along with the others, is suspended for five days. David tells him he can go fuck himself. Hector gulps. "Five days," he repeats.

David lifts his muscle shirt to reveal a gun tucked into the front of his pants. "I'll take three days," then lets his shirt fall to conceal the gun once again.

Hector takes in a deep breath. "No, David. Five days."

At this point, three members of our security team walk slowly toward the scene. It ignites David: "I'll smoke you and all your fuckin' security guards."

This moves Hector to swing around and scream, "GET THE FUCK AWAY FROM HERE!" They back up completely.

When Hector wheels around, David is on the phone. It's never good when homies, during some confrontation, get on the phone. More often than not, the enraged one is calling for backup. David tries to enter the back building, and Hector blocks him. "I can't let you in there with that gun." Hector then surmises that David must have been "drinking hard stuff" because he is getting progressively drunker in his presence. He marvels at the delayed reaction of it all as David slurs his speech and becomes even more wobbly.

David unleashes a torrent of invective and Hector feels this great churning in his stomach. His entire body is sending him this message: *You are going to die now.* In the telling of this story years later, he reflects at that moment: "I knew it would be a good death." He feels at peace. "It wouldn't have been a bad death, like from my years on the streets, gangbanging." He's resigned himself to this.

David leaves. Later that evening, he bumps into the cops, they find the gun, and he ends up going to prison.

Two years later David walks into Homeboy and approaches Hector in the reception area. Hector inhales deeply. "I want to apologize to you for what happened," David says. "I hope you'll forgive me. And . . . I want to know if I can have another chance?"

Hector embraces him. "Welcome home, David. We've been waiting for you." Don't erase the board so soon.

It was the large family gatherings that underscored the wound. Sammy would notice that all his little cousins had a father's knee to sit on. He would play it off that he was too old or too cool and had no need of anyone's knee. His lament and rage, however, was mainly on his kid brother's behalf. He needed a knee. It was not until years later that he recognized this vague ache that seemed to saturate his long-ing and occasionally short-circuit his own flourishing. Sammy found a way, in walking with others, to do what the Buddhists say: "Tend to the part of the garden you can reach." He could reach the ache and welcome it. He let it be light to bring clarity to so much.

All of Miguel's older siblings were in foster care already. His mom had a brief respite from her addiction, long enough for baby Miguel to stay in her care. By the two-month mark, his mom was arrested for a very large amount of cocaine—kilos and kilos—and Miguel was also swept up and put in a foster home until he was two years old. "I was abused in that house. Though I was tiny, I remember this woman putting a hot iron on me." He was volleyed to many places after that.

When he was ten, he returned to his mother, who again had achieved some short-lived bout of recovery and remained jail-free. All his other sibs had been adopted out. By age fourteen, his mother had returned to a constant state of getting high. Food wasn't even put on the table. Miguel was arguing with her in the passenger seat of the car, promising he would now go to Child Protective Services to report her. He got out of the car, and before he could reach the side-walk, "She ranned me over." This sent him to the hospital with severe head injuries. His mother was mandated to prison for two years.

So many more years passed before Miguel could settle into com-fort with himself. After the birth of his son and several violent out-bursts at Homeboy, he went to rehab and has now allowed himself to be held in a community where wounds can close. Relationship itself. We are called to belong to the Beloved, and we walk with each other in a constant state of reminder. We invite others to belonging and remind them of this long-standing invitation. It's what we all try to model.

I don't know the homie sitting in front of me. I don't think he has taken a *playa* in a minute, and he looks bereft. His tattoos alone say that he qualifies to be here with us. He shows me a large bandage on his right arm, where days before he had been stabbed at a Metro station. "I almost bled to death, until someone found me and called for help." He seems as tired as a soul can be. I write the note indicating "Drug test any Friday at 10:00" and give it to him.

"Now, don't lose this," I tell him. "It's how they'll know I've approved you." I hand him the note, folded, with my card and "40 bones" tucked in there. I tell him, "You will love it here, and we'll love you back." Who can explain fully the convergence of things, but he just dissolves in tears. When he can look up at me from this crying bout, he says, "I'm gonna bring my light here."

"Please do," I tell him. "We could use it." I am so heartened that he knows he has light. It's a good place to start.

Oscar has a searing memory from when he was five. His mom places him on the couch, along with his kid brother, and puts a video on. It's *A Nightmare on Elm Street*. Oscar is planted there, his brother sound asleep, while his mother goes into the bedroom. Oscar takes in every frightening image and keeps his eyes transfixed on the disfigured midnight mangler, Freddy Krueger. The only light filling the living room comes from the terror on the TV.

Before long, Oscar hears great crashing sounds of things being thrown in his parents' room. He morphs the monster on the screen with the sounds coming from the bedroom and quickly convinces himself that Freddy Krueger is now in that room, causing the mayhem. He stays riveted, with his spine pushed up against the back of the couch, paralyzed in fear. It doesn't jar him into some action, but rather into a stillness and terrified anticipation. The mounting noises reach a climax, and his mom bolts from the room, naked and with an absolutely petrified face. "I'll never forget her terrified look." He waits breathlessly for Freddy to emerge from the room, pursuing his mom outside, where she has fled. "But then my father ran out of the room. And I realized that it was my father who was chasing my mom. I discovered that night . . . that my father was the monster."

"I was afraid of everything after that," Oscar told me. Everything seemed to make him anxious, and all he remembered was unmitigated dread. His aunts invited him to Disneyland once. He said no. He was too frightened. His father forced him to fight in the backyard with his cousins, and his fear to do so was apparent. "No real man is ever afraid," his father would scream at him.

Then his all-pervasive dread was replaced by a terror of "not being a real man." He said many years later, "This stirred a conflict in me." He learned to fight. He had developed a bad stutter that accompanied his constantly anxious self. He was teased and bullied. Finally, the day would come and he'd say to the bully, "Come here—I fight better than I speak." He eventually went to prison at seventeen, sentenced to fifty years for his involvement in a murder. He would later receive a commutation from Governor Brown and was released after fifteen years.

Oscar wandered through our doors, but he struggled to find sure footing at Homeboy. Stevie told him once, "Dawg, your car can't go forward until you get it out of reverse." After hiccups, starts and stops, and endless two steps forward and three steps back, Oscar found a way to brilliantly go into the dark and not be consumed by it anymore. He found some soul retrieval as he was held in love by simply everyone. He was cherished into a return to his self, a journey he never thought he'd make. He said once, "You can't judge a guy by his book." True enough.

I wouldn't be able to unpack Robert Sapolsky's critique of free will. He wrote a whole book on it. As a biologist and neuroscientist, he suggests that life "without free will" as a notion might be more generous and, indeed, reverent of human complexity. A stance at the margins. Anyone trekking to the margins knows that for a very long time, life for someone like Oscar has been about being blamed and punished and deprived and ignored for things over which he had no control. I suspect Sapolsky is quite right that humanity has been saddled with great misery due to the myths of free will. It's liberating to consider this, as it can permit real affectionate awe where it would, indeed, be helpful.

I suppose what divides us is not about ideas that people hold. It's about fears that people have. It's why we cross the street to avoid folks like Oscar. But when we learn to bow and to look with attention, we can inaugurate a fresh movement and then choose to abide in it. If we just stay on the side of the street where human beings walk, we have a chance at beholding preciousness. Loving humility gives rise to affection for those who carry so much and yet are still willing to give their last dollar and only shirt.

VISIBLE ENTIRELY

MARY OLIVER ENCOURAGES US TO "BE WHERE YOU ARE IN THE universe" and to "start the day in happiness, in kindness." I have tried to calibrate my daily intentionality to greet people . . . and to choose to brighten. It's not just about smiling (though that's a good place to start). It's about greeting, truly seeing people, and finding yourself anchored in the sure and certain knowledge that "the only non-delusional response to everything is kindness," as George Saunders reminds us. Which is also to say that every other response is delusional. Our rage, resentment, relentless annoyance, impatience . . . all delusional. Kindness lets us brighten and greet folks. It changes everything. When you greet people in this way, watch folks revive. The heart gets jump-started. Yours and theirs.

My friend, the U.S. surgeon general Dr. Vivek Murthy, has underscored loneliness as a pervasive health issue in our country and proposes a national framework to rebuild social connection and community in America. A great many health experts say that loneliness can be as hazardous to your health as smoking. What Murthy highlights that is so helpful and connects with life here in the Homeboy Industries community is that, essentially, loneliness is not about being alone, but largely about belonging. Above all, healing is different from "fixing." Our belonging involves everyone in the healing process. All hands on deck are needed to undo aloneness. To become whole and aid others in this effort, we all dedicate ourselves to constant listening and learning and abiding in love. Letting our hearts be altered by each other. One decides to let love live through you. We seek to build a world dedicated to healing with kindness as a constant and radical act of defiance.

Stevie says, "At Homeboy, folks heal on steroids." I overheard a homie giving a tour: "Here at Homeboy, if you're struggling and really going through it, they don't just say, 'Go into a room and figure it out.' They're in the room with us."

Another homie chimed in, shadowing this tour guide: "At Homeboy, you reach out for help and a million hands reach back to you."

In my office with an African American gang member who was at Homeboy for the first time, I tell him, "People love each other here."

He looks at me, then glances out to the reception area. "Yeah, you don't have to tell it . . . you feel it." We are all alone together.

The traumatized are encased in the defended self. Every dose that everyone here dispenses seems to say, "Rely on my faith in you, until you have your own." As is said around here often: "Try kindness. And if that doesn't work, increase the dose." Until the armor welded around your heart comes undone. This requires constant attention—which is a good definition of prayer. We are invited to practice heaven always in this attention to what's right in front of us.

Chuy tells me his prayer is constant gratitude "for what God's done" and "for what he's workin' on." Chuy seems to know in his very depths that God is a direction in which our grateful hearts lean. He tells me how he brings to his prayerful attention all his enemies and his "exes." He brings to prayerful mindfulness his parents, who he says are "drug-mental." Chuy finds himself—the very generosity of God. He texts me: "God is so good, Poppa. I didn't know that all these years." This realization allows him "to be in that room" while we all, together, try to figure it out.

I took the Carranza brothers, Joseph and Oscar, to New York City and Syracuse. We have exactly twenty minutes between arriving at Gate 19C at Midway Airport to book it to the absolute farthest gate for our flight to Syracuse. "Let's go." I'm dragging my bag, moving quickly, and the brothers are close behind. I think, *How does an old person make these connections?* Then I realize: *I* AM AN OLD PERSON!!

We get to the farthest reaches of the airport and of my stress threshold. We arrive at the gate. Oscar, the younger brother, ducks into the restroom. Joseph is resting his hands on his knees, panting and beaming with delight. He's a scrappy, tattooed twenty-six-year-old. He's just beaming, positively giddy and exhilarated. "This is amazing, G. I've never experienced anything like it. I mean, the vibe here . . . everybody running to their planes. Most incredible experience of my life." I'm stupefied by all this. He continues, "You know what the soundtrack of my heart is right now?"

"No," I tell him.

"I'm so excited," he sings, and does a little *cholo* jig. And he "just can't hiiiide it." He's being where he is in the universe. Rumi asks,

135

"What still pulls on your soul?" For Joseph, just starting his day with happiness does. Again, as Mary Oliver writes, "Holiness is visible, entirely." Even in our frantic mad dashes.

Joseph taught me about joy that morning. He reminded me to remember that joy is a decision. It doesn't drop out of the sky and land in your lap. You choose it. Later that evening, when I reflected this moment back to him, he said, "Here and now ... is the only thing that matters." We practice heaven, here in the room. So we try to find the infinite in every moment. Needless to say, our deepest union with God happens in the present moment, so we might as well stay there. Someone asked Yogi Berra for the time, and he said, "You mean right now?" Yes. Right now. Practicing heaven right now. Only then can we discover "what God's workin' on."

The goal of dosing with brightness is to help each other find wholeness. At Homeboy, I suppose what we're doing is creating an atmosphere where nonduality and interdependence can be palpably experienced. Good relationships keep us afloat, thriving, and happy. We don't want to run out of them. It is proven that isolated loneliness leads to a shorter life and great unhappiness. The intriguing documentary *Penguin Town* states that penguins' "survival depends on strong relationships." With us, too. Wholeness is akin to what Thich Nhat Hanh says of enlightenment: "The wave does not need to die to become water. She is already water." Wholeness happens when the wave knows it's the ocean. Or, as CVS advertises: "Healthier Happens Together." Connection. Even in small doses, it has a cumulative impact.

Lencho and Kiko are working behind the counter at Homegirl Café. The lunch rush is over, and they are cleaning up and talking with Lola, one of their coworkers. Lola's phone rings as they're "choppin' it up." "REALLY?" she says to the caller. "That's awful," she continues. "I don't know; let me ask." She turns to Lencho and Kiko: "Either of you know what to do if a tree falls on your car?"

Lencho jumps right in: "First, get the tree's information. All of it . . . roots . . . everything." Healthier happens together.

The magnificent Scott Santarosa, once pastor at Dolores Mission Church and my superior (and later Provincial), would greet me in the morning with our coffee, and one of us would say to the other, "Give us this day your daily dread." We would mine our upcoming schedule that day and find the odious task to which neither of us was looking forward. We settle for happiness when we should hold out for joy. Our longing was to welcome the dreaded thing. If only happiness is the goal, it diminishes our tolerance for the dreadful and those things that distress us daily. All the worst adult coping mechanisms merely seek to numb our dread. Our goal, instead, is to be curious about the distress. We let it in, and we become more sturdy as we welcome it. We don't eliminate it, but we can watch it be relieved of its power.

We drug test at Homeboy. We didn't always. It became clear that this was necessary to give folks a goal before beginning with us, and it kept us vigilant with trainees who would slip and relapse. If people are facing things and coming to terms with what has happened to them, the temptation to numb is high. With the changing laws regarding marijuana, however, we needed to moderate our response some. Folks all smoke bud, no matter how one tries to dissuade them.

"Okay," I ask two homies, "give me the benefits of blazing it."

The pair of them use their fingers to count off the many ways. One says, "It relaxes you."

The other: "It gives you the munchies."

They get stalled. I help them. "It gets you stuck on stupid." If one of our prospective trainees tests dirty for marijuana, we still bring them in, but we test them again in thirty days. If the level is lower, we move them from part-time to full-time. If not, they stay put where they are. The hope is that they are clear-eyed and attentive to the ocean to which we all belong.

Nearly forty-five years ago, I had the oddest and most extensive bout of insomnia ever. It was one of the happiest times in my life. I was studying philosophy at Gonzaga University. I loved my Jesuit community, had lots of friends, gave retreats, was in plays, opened a soup kitchen on the weekends with a Jesuit buddy, and would regularly get lost in the "Bermuda Triangle" of the Bulldog tavern or the Forum or Jack and Dan's. All we did was laugh. And I couldn't sleep. This went on for weeks. Initially, I was enjoying myself so much that there was this low-grade exhilaration that kept me sleepless in Spokane. Then, as the wide-awake evenings turned into many days, bedtime was my daily dread. Eyes wide-open, staring at the ceiling and fearing the evening every day. Finally, I couldn't take it anymore. I knocked on the door of a very wise old Jesuit, Mike Pastizzo, who lived in my house. I relayed the depth of my dread and distress. He said just one thing: "What are you afraid of?" I spent some minutes on this, wanting to say the most truthful thing I could land on.

"I'm afraid," I tell him, "that I will never sleep again." He nearly comes to his feet. "GOOD!! Now pray for that . . . long, and wish for that. Ask God to give you this wonderful gift, to never sleep again." So that night, I did. Fell sound asleep, after nearly three weeks of nuthin'.

Give us this day our daily dread. Thank you, sir, I'll have another.

I'm giving a series of talks at Lakeside Chautauqua, Ohio. It's a little village with a storied history spanning over a hundred years.

Toward the end of the week, an elderly woman spots me, crosses the street, points at me, and says, "You." I stop. She continues. "For five days now, YOU ... have ... held ... us ..."

I say, "Hostage."

We both laugh. Total strangers. We get a dose of something oddly relational. We never even got to what I presume was going to be a compliment. We walk on. I suspect we both felt like waves ... quite at one with the ocean.

All of us await some permission to imagine things looking different. What galvanizes our imagination is the permission to see as a goal, for example, the day when policing is obsolete and our prisons are empty. When there is no more "human caging." We begin in the acknowledgment that the U.S. has only 5 percent of the world's population, but one quarter of its prisoners. We allow ourselves to see the day when police are guardians and not warriors. It's perfectly fine to imagine this and acknowledge that our nation has built and blessed and normalized the largest system of punishment and imprisonment in the history of human civilization. Recognizing that is a start. We can see that prisons are places of monumental disregard for the human person AND a place where there is superhuman resilience to this very large indifference.

A tribal lawyer I met in Montana told me: "We put folks in prison because we're mad at them, not because they're a danger." Our goal is not to create nicer prisons, but healthier communities. "Healthier happening together" can even tackle mass incarceration. We realize that in isolation, hope dims, but in a community of cherished belonging, our hope flourishes and thrives. It's okay to imagine it.

Truth be told, we have always rushed to incarcerate. Generations of poor kids of color have been placed at a distance from belonging, and we can recognize how that has torn apart the social fabric of our communities. We can see now that more punishment has never increased public safety. They say that two-thirds of everyone in jail has mental health problems, but anyone close to the justice-involved knows this figure is too low. This in no way stigmatizes but frees us to direct our cherishing dosage toward those in a broken place. No longer would we ever say, "bad people go to jail," but, rather, now, "wounded, not yet whole people" do.

The first juvenile court in the United States was established in 1899, because it dawned on people that minors would be less morally culpable than adults. Yet none of it has to do with morality, but, rather, health and wholeness. Neuroscience shows us that cherishing activates the prefrontal cortex. So brain science and the true sense of rehabilitation reveal clearly that it is healthy folks who have impulse control, not moral folks.

Homies often say, "I just want to get right with God."

I tell them, "When were you ever wrong with God?"

It is never about "righting the moral compass" but tending to the wound.

Homies, especially those who have served long sentences, will often say, "We are used to being watched, but aren't used to being seen." The poet Ada Limón tells us that we are "made whole, by being not a witness, but witnessed." Not just Homeboy, but every community we nurture into being wants to be a safe place where people are seen and then are cherished. Stevie often says, "Our culture will keep us safe." In Papua, New Guinea, there is no word for "hello." One greets someone by saying, "You are here." It is answered with "Yes, I am."

Every morning meeting at Homeboy begins with someone reading the land acknowledgment, that we are standing on the land of the Tongva. A homie, Jarvis, points out, "Yeah, we read the land acknowledgment, but we are all also . . . acknowledged here." You are here. You are being witnessed.

Homies are famous for their ability to call up nicknames that perfectly capture the person. In an odd way, it heightens our "seeing" of each other. There was a homie who looked exactly like John Wayne and so he was dubbed. There was a kid born with a condition that enlarged his right forearm. His homies call him Popeye. Another was born with his left forearm missing. He is crowned Lefty. The naming enhances our belonging and declares that "you are a part of us." This always feels undeniable when I see it.

In the early days of the Homeboy Bakery, Manuel was in charge of getting the homies to bake bread. A man in his sixties, he could speak only Spanish and he knew everything about baking. He could dip his mitt in a huge vat of dough and knew if it was right and had the perfect level of moisture. The homies drove him crazy because he wasn't used to "corralling," which became central to his job description. Manuel would fly into a panic and holler at the homies to bring this tray, pull the bread out of the oven, don't add any more water to that dough. He was loved and respected, essentially, but his bakers were a handful.

Omar was the most hardheaded of the lot, and Manuel exerted most of his energy trying to get him to actually perform the necessary tasks. He'd yell at Omar to turn that, do this, stir the vat, and Omar would constantly and calmly say to Manuel, waving his hand, "Ya Ya." "Ya Ya" is the moral equivalent of "I'll get to it . . . eventually." This response would give a huge apoplectic jolt to Manuel's blood pressure and he would yell back, 'YA YA NO!!!" And a nickname was born.

No baker ever called him Manuel again. When one of our bakers, Roman, was gunned down, "Ya Ya No" led the procession of Roman's coworkers, wearing white aprons, from the bakery across the street to the church. Ya Ya No carried a perfectly round artisanal loaf at the time of the offertory at Roman's funeral mass. For all the aggravation and the spikes of Manuel's blood pressure, there was so much affection shared among them all for this grizzled old baker. And he held these *cabezones* with tenderness, and all their survival and flourishing depended on it. When Manuel died some years ago, the homie bakers in attendance at his funeral tearfully invoked Ya Ya No and remembered how the birth of a nickname can, in fact, make us whole in being "witnessed."

The most pronounced Scripture passage from 1 Corinthians 13 ends with "Love never fails." I also like another translation that renders it: "Love never stops loving." Still, the First Nations translation puts it this way: "The road to love has no end." The addition of the road as a notion is helpful here. Or, as Sergio underscores: "Love is never a false doctrine" and "Love won't let us go."

I thought I was alone in our office. It was 5:30 p.m. and everyone had left for the day. This was in our old headquarters, which had been an upholstery shop. There were two restrooms in the reception area. I was about to lock up when Gabriel and Jessica come out of the men's room. They looked stunned. I exclaimed, "Hello??!!" with a decided tone, laced with WTF. Jessica is a lesbian and quite masculine. She is a tough homegirl and well tattooed. Gabriel is an innocent in the world, though his stocky, tattooed self might suggest otherwise.

"Pops," Gabriel began to explain in his rapid-fire way, more accelerated than usual. "It's just that Jessica asked me to do her some hickies."

Jessica grabbed the baton. "I wanted to make Karla [her girl-friend] jealous, so I asked him to do me that *paro*." Jessica's neck was spotted with *chupetonazos*. No greater love than this. The road to love has no end.

We choose, then, love as our practice. Practice doesn't ever make perfect; it makes permanent. If not permanent, then increasingly habitual. Second nature. This is how we inhabit our dignity and nobility in each other's presence, and this is exquisitely mutual and eternally replenishing. A wise homie told me once, "We need to find each other in one another." This requires some surrender to the place.

A senior staff homie says: "At Homeboy, you don't have to dance with everybody, but ya gotta dance with somebody." Disappoint-ment, failure, and half-heartedness do not speak this language. Only surrender does. It maintains only tender delight and abiding admira-tion. You then find your joy and fearlessness in walking on the road with those who are left out. You look with attention and greet with a thrill. Ya gotta dance with somebody.

Jarvis and Solomon are standing behind me in the Southwest Air-lines A boarding group. I catch Jarvis whispering to Solomon, "This your first time flying with Pops?"

"Yeah," he tells him.

"Me too," in an even softer tone. They both have this habit of beginning every sentence with "I ain't gonna lie . . ." and then they complete the sentence. "I ain't gonna lie . . . there's nuthin' to do here in Odessa." Or "I ain't gonna lie . . . I think we're the only two Black folks in town." Or "I ain't gonna lie . . . since there's nuthin' to do . . . maybe we can go cow tippin.'"

Like that. They wow every audience. They're introduced at one venue as "icons of possibility." To this day, I call Jarvis "the mayor of

Odessa." Suddenly, people are able to trade in a doomy narrative for a roomy one. When that happens, everyone feels a little less invisible. Nothing passive here. I ain't gonna lie.

We choose to brighten, so that we can cherish with every breath and find ourselves alive and thriving, flourishing in relational wholeness. When 2 Corinthians tells us "God loves a cheerful giver," Saint Paul is not asking us to be perky or even to be thankful to God. It's a recognition that, indeed, WE ARE the generosity of God. Our brightening with each other finds a full participation in that. It enhances our benevolence so that our goal is not our own happiness but another's happiness.

Richard calls me and wants me to be the first to know that his son has just entered the world. He's holding him in his arms, and I'm touched that he'd think to call me. "Damn, G . . . this fool's got a gang o' fur." I can visualize him sitting in the hospital room's recliner while his lady is asleep in the bed. Richard worked at Homeboy but now has moved beyond and settled into a good job while simultaneously leaving behind the gang madness. He's a sharp and quick-witted twenty-year-old whose sense of humor goes to the quirky and very smart. I ask him if he was there when the baby was born. Sometimes the homies aren't.

"Yeah," he says, "I was there when my lady went 'Pop Goes the Weasel.'" I can hear the baby, in the background, making gurgling sounds. I ask him about the experience of being there when his son was born. "It was VERY painful, G. My lady would *pinche* this and *pinche* that, and she called me *cabrón* a gang o' times and she kept digging her fingernails into my arm the WHOLE time. Yeah, it was very painful. WAY more painful for ME than it was for her." I make him promise never to share these sentiments with his lady.

I move us to another emotional register, beyond his silliness, and tell him how proud I am. "I can remember you running up to cars, selling crack, dropping out of school, packing a *cuete*, never going home, down for your barrio. And now look at you. You're a working man, a loving husband, you never come to the projects. You dedicate your life to this growing family and this son of yours, who is the luckiest kid alive to have you as his dad. I hope you're as proud of yourself as I am of you."

Silence. For several beats. Silence. Then he says, "Hey, G, this fool just said 'hi' to you. No, wait . . . Never mind . . . He just farted." You greet with a thrill and hope for a contagion of benevolence. "Holiness visible entirely." It always shows up.

There is a famous story about a Zen master who was asked about the highest teaching of Zen. He wrote the word "Attention" on the blackboard.

The student persisted and asked, "But isn't there anything else?"

The master said, "Yes, there is," and once again, he wrote the word "Attention" on the blackboard.

The student insisted, "There must be something more."

And his teacher turned to the board and wrote yet another time, "Attention." Now the board announced, "Attention. Attention. Attention." It is all that is required, since attention will always bring us back to the present. We are continually saved in the present moment.

Pádraig Ó Tuama says that prayer is greeting. He suggests that it is a training ground for the curiosity we'll need when we choose to pay attention to each other. We dive right into the very generous hospitality of God, in the present moment, by consciously greeting folks. It is how we pray without ceasing. The constant attention of prayer is an invitation to practice heaven always, attentive to the person who's right in front of us.

JayCee and Edgar are helping me speak to a bunch of educators in a Utah ski resort. It's a massive, sprawling place, and as we move through it, it's hard for the homies to keep up with my brisk pace. I suspect that, to them, moving quickly is just decidedly uncool. Nevertheless, I plow through this expansive resort with quickness. I constantly have to turn to Edgar and ask, "Where's JayCee?"

And Edgar, with great eye-rolling, turns and points to JayCee, at a distance, stopped in his tracks, chatting up a group of folks. "Running for president," he says. Relax. He's choosing to brighten. He's paying attention.

The prophet Ezekial says, "The spirit entered me and set me on my feet." God's loving energy in the world is to lift us up, set us on our feet. God is a God who loves through all loving. I suppose we settle, sometimes, for being laid out, on the ground, low down, if you will. Carl Rogers says it's not just about accepting people but prizing them. God sets us on our feet, not just to stand but so that we can move forward and walk each other home. Beyond understanding each other, we begin to believe in each other. Healthy people know where the joy is and how to prize the gift in the other.

Trayvon is released from prison after twenty-three years. He was a juvenile tried as an adult. He is four days out when he shows up at Homeboy and sits down in front of my desk. He's a gang member who has done lengthy time in prison, so he qualifies to enter our eighteen-month program. The process to begin starts with a drug test, then a week later an orientation (to see if Trayvon wants into this program), and a week after that, an interview with the selection committee, all made up of homies and homegirls.

We had never met, and it is the first time he has ever set foot in our headquarters. He is demonstrably nervous. He tells me so, but his near hyperventilating preceded his admission. We're human beings. Fretting and anxiety seem to come with the equipment, but Trayvon is in nervous overdrive. I try to calm him down as I write on a piece of paper, "Drug test any Friday at 10." This will be his "pass" to show at the front desk to begin the process. (I told a homegirl to come and drug test any Friday at 10. As she was leaving my office, she says, "So . . . I have to wait and urinate on Friday?" Since this was a Monday, I told her best not to wait.)

"So," I ask him, "how'd ya hear about Homeboy?" I continue to write the note.

"Oh, some female told me." I keep writing. "Yeah," he continues, "She said you fathered all her children."

I stop writing. A meerkat lifting its head. "Say what, now?" I ask.

Trayvon seems to be watching the very words he just uttered as they float above my desk. "Wait, that's not right . . . you BAPTIZED all her children."

"Oh," I tell him, "that's a bit different." We fall over ourselves laughing. I tell him to skip the drug test. I rip up the piece of paper. "You start tomorrow." The whole moment, bristling with nervous tension, sets us both on our feet, inhabiting our joy to walk each other home. Alive and thriving, glad for each other's company.

What every human and, in a special way, returning citizen seeks is what the Christmas carol calls "comfort and joy." In that order. At Homeboy, we offer a safe place that becomes in a heartbeat "comfort."

Many years ago, Cara walks into my office filled with gang members, and I can tell she needs to talk about something. Cara was a Jesuit volunteer who stayed on for ten years with us. I ask the homies, "Hey, can I have my office so Cara and I can talk?" All the homies leave, but one, Ralphie, doesn't budge. I stare at him.

He says calmly, "Anything you have to say to Cara . . . you can say to me."

And like my dad and Oliver Hardy, I say, "Would ya get your ass outta . . ." He hightails it. His comfort. Our joy. Both of each.

Edgar calls. "Hey, G, you think ya can pick me up?"

"I think I can," I tell him.

"Well, then be the little engine that could . . . and get your ass over here." This is banter not from an uncomfortable place, but one that is safe at home. I took my sweet time getting there.

Once, I was doing battle with traffic, trying to get to some gig on time. I had three homies in tow. José was sitting shotgun and was providing constant correctives to my freeway negotiating. He was a backseat driver, but he was seated up front. After repeating "Watch out" and "Slow down," just as I was about to tell him that I've been driving decades before his parents even met, he said, "You're an offensive driver. I like that."

I turned to him and said, "You're an offensive passenger. Not crazy about it." We got it like that. When he proposes some idea in a meeting and I really don't like it, there is no sugarcoating. "Wow . . . that's a bad idea."

He'll stare at me and say, "You just shot me down, like a big-nosed clown." Our comfort IS our joy.

I enter the restroom while active drug testing is taking place. Mario has blue latex gloves on, and a nervous prospective homie trainee stands, in front of the sink, awaiting his instructions. I greet them and make my way to the urinal. "You know," Mario tells this guy, "we no longer do UAs; we don't have you piss in a cup here." I sense Mario is performing for an audience of one. "Yeah, now we do . . . anal swabs."

From my post, I clarify: "DON'T BELIEVE HIM." All of this is not a far cry from Ubuntu: "A person is only a person through other persons." And, yes, comfort and joy.

If Damon Runyon were still alive and writing about gang members, he'd feature Cuco. He is one of our stalwart security guys. Huge and maybe imposing on first bounce. Been to prison, savvy, but has a keen sense of people. "Each of us," Pope Francis says, "is fully a person when we are part of a people." Cuco knows how to welcome and to what he is welcoming folks: "a people." He ushers a nervous young gang member into my office. He does this when he sniffs out young folks who are apprehensive. He shows him the seat in front of my desk. "Keep your hands where I can see 'em and don't touch nuthin'." It's a routine I've watched for a very long time. It always works. For an instant, we all feel "fully a person."

I suppose at Homeboy we are always seeking full human flourishing. *Eudaemonia* is a contented state of being happy, healthy, and prosperous. It has nothing to do with bank accounts. Aristotle thought it was the highest human good. I would call it "flourishing joy." Ignatius spoke of *cura personalis*—a care for the whole person. This involves healthy physical development, sound psychological growth, and life-sustaining spiritual formation. Frank Buckley, a Jesuit therapist at Homeboy, calls it the 5 F's: Faith, Fitness, Focus, Food, and Friends. Overall, this sees health, really, as wholeness. Nothing is left out. It seeks completion in the well-being of body, mind, and spirit. It doesn't settle for insight. The Buddhists speak of the "uprightness of heart." It means a virtuous person. In other words, a healthy one. A person longing for "flourishing joy."

We seek to help folks become, more and more, their truth in love by loving them, by choosing to brighten, and this builds loving societies. Systems change when people do. People change when they are cherished. We propel our intentions away from our own self-absorption, and we choose to forget ourselves on purpose. Our awakened heart sees that everyone gleams with the splendor of God, and being a constant reminder is our joy. Living life fully is what Zen Buddhists call "the supreme meal," a life without limits. Our habitual practice, and our choosing to cherish with every breath, is a decision not to break faith with our awakened heart. We choose to live, all over again, and daily, at the solitary core of our being. We abide in the oneness and in the longing... in the love that rests within us. In this, again, we realize that all human longing and desire is just love trying to happen.

Cherishing people is easy. Remembering to cherish is really difficult. A woman emailed me, recounting how exasperating it is to love her siblings. "They don't push my buttons—they install them." (I saw a T-shirt in a San Francisco window: "I'm sorry that I pushed all your buttons . . . but I was looking for the mute.") A homie told me that he decided to stay home and "take a mental health day. So, I stayed home. But by 8:15 I knew I had to get my ass back to Homeboy . . . because Homeboy feeds my spirit. It IS where I find mental health. I feel the bond here. I can't help it . . . it's my happy place." It is to this place of health and wholeness that we choose to brighten and walk. Where buttons are neither installed nor pushed.

Joey remembers his dad waking him up in the middle of the night. He's maybe in the third grade; he has school tomorrow. His dad would put him on the handlebars of his bike. They would ride to the train station. The two would scour the floor for cigarette butts. The father made a game of this. When they found a mostly complete cigarette, they'd come home. Joey spoke of his mom who left them: "She wasn't able to maintain her relationship with my dad."

Later, Joey writes to me from Juvenile Hall, "My tears are my only food." He finds his way to prison and writes me earnestly: "In my next life, I'm doing things right. Promise I'll go to school . . . think more." Much later, when Joey finally walks through our doors, he comes to know how receiving love is transformational. It enables him to come alive to things and people and himself. Shirley Torres, director of programs, says, "If you're not feeling, you're not healing." Joey is healing. His homies had always called him Sniper. Soon, he'd correct people. "Call me by my government name." After a heavy-duty crying jag with me, we end our conversation and he hugs me: "You're the fucking greatest." When he finally releases me from this *abrazo*, he looks me in the eye and says, "And *spensa*, for saying 'fucking greatest.'"

Because I'm a geezer, I had to ask a homie what a FAQ was. I know. But there is one frequently asked question of me by homies: "Did you get my text?" The texts are constant. It is hard to keep up. When I'm in the office, I don't really have time to glance at my phone. So, in the very long walk from my desk to the restroom, homies will pass me in the hallway and ask, "Did you get my text?"

Huero sent me one: "The guy who runs this halfway house was advising me to be a little less amicable." I text back (eventually): "You can never be TOO amicable." He writes: "That's what I'm trying to say. LOL. But sometimes, I guess, certain personalities are just too big for the world." We aspire to this. But connection is what we strive for and what helps us find our way to joy.

Homegirl Inez says, "Connect to everything. Attach to nothing." We are like penguins in this regard. We can't survive without it. Even as I write these words, right now, in a crummy flat in London, a homie texts me: "I just heard you had died. I'm texting to see if it's true." I thank him and say, "I'm texting from heaven. The cell service here is amazing."

Our second "headquarters" was a storefront on First Street. It has a reception area of sorts. Two very old couches placed in an L shape with a low coffee table in the middle. There is no air conditioning, so we keep the front door open during the summer but we can never achieve real climate comfort. I am rushing out to somewhere, and two homies who work here are seated on the couches, feet up on the coffee table, eating Popsicles on an exceedingly hot summer day. I stop before leaving and stare them down. "I wish I had a job where I could put my feet up and eat Popsicles all day."

One homie turns to the other and says, "Hey . . . that's the job *we* have."

We had spoken in Jersey City at Saint Peter's Prep in the morning and at Saint Peter's University at night. I have Louis and Fabian with me, and they are old shoes. I have a comfort level with them born of so many years and a history of struggle. Both were addicts for a long time; now they are wise figures of sobriety. At our current headquarters, Louis, a big fella, once tackled a gang member who was extremely high on PCP after the guy brandished a gun and aimed it at him. It all ended well, and (eventually) an apology was uttered, but both Louis and Fabian were deserving of combat pay. Maybe in the next life. Comfort and joy in this one.

Both the institutions we spoke at are run by the Jesuits. We spend the night in the university's Jesuit community. We are set to leave the morning after our evening talk, and we sit with an old Jesuit at breakfast before our departure. Very generously, the Jesuit says, "Let's go now to the campus store so you can pick out sweatshirts and stuff. After all," he says proudly, "we are the home of the Peacocks."

These two already did a similar run on the campus store at the

Prep the day before, and I think they have more than enough swag to bring home. "Hey, many thanks, but we need to get to the airport."

As we walk to our rental car, towing our bags, Louis turns to me and says, "I can't believe you. 'We don't have time to go to the campus store'?" Then he glares at me. "Motherfucking Peacock blocker." Maybe I've laughed as hard as this exact moment before, but if I have, I can't remember it. Do you have the time? You mean right now?

No one is sure what happened to Isaiah, but he is lying in an ICU with many bullet wounds to his chest. In his first three days in the hospital, he's already endured two long surgeries. He's a homie at our Youth Re-entry Center and a student at our school, Learning Works at Homeboy. I took him on a trip to Salt Lake City with his mentor and case manager, Tee. In anticipation of his first flight, Isaiah is the kind of nervous that turns giggly and hyper. He would laugh and do odd kinds of jigs. I watch at LAX as he frenetically wanders into the women's restroom and chart on my watch how long it will take for him to realize and exit.

I go to the exit row on Southwest, and Isaiah and Tee follow. The flight attendant has an odd freakout moment. "How old are you?" she asks Isaiah. He says eighteen, and she asks to see his ID. He looks twelve. He is a tad miffed as the flight attendant leaves earshot distance. "Damn, I got my chin hairs growing." Like this would be proof enough for anybody. Isaiah inhabits an unfamiliar person in his talks: himself. He discovers that his journey is luminous and people can see by it. After our several days on the road, in the car returning to Homeboy, he confides, "I'd rather represent Homeboy than a gang."

"Why?" I ask him.

"'Cuz . . . Homeboy's got purpose."

A group from the Youth Re-Entry community goes to visit Isaiah, and one texts me an update on his condition: "Even with the tubes and all and he couldn't speak, he did manage to give us a thumbs-up AND the middle finger. So, I think he's outta the woods." Isaiah has been having nightmares, I'm told. Though he also has a dream that I come to him and tell him all will be well. Those students and staff surrounding his bed join God in living infinitely in love with us. Everyone finds themselves, in such an act of surrounding, awakened to what is already there. It is what we mean when we say "the self, hidden with Christ in God." Beyond the ego and our own brokenness, we find this holiness in our being whole together. Healthier happening in comfort and flourishing joy. Increase the dose.

7

MAKE WINDOWS

THE TWO OF THEM HAVE NEVER HAD A STEAK BEFORE. I SUPPOSE they've had carne asada, but they've never ordered a steak in a restaurant. "This is our first time," Glen says as he waves at the plates before him and his "lady," Cynthia. Glen hasn't been out a year yet, after having spent thirty years in prison, a juvenile tried as an adult. Cynthia's smile shimmers as the two deem the steaks delicious, even after she was dubious at ordering one medium. "I just don't want them bloody," Cynthia insisted.

At dessert time, Cynthia peers at the menu and wants to know what a lava cake is. Before I can tell her, Glen gives a perfect description of the liquid chocolate core within this small, round chocolate cake. I ask him if he's ever had one before. He tells me no. "My cellie and me, every night, we'd make our coffee, split a honeybun, then watch the cooking show on PBS. We'd also watch *Globe Trekker*.

We'd go to Morocco, see the Great Wall of China, and we'd imagine, one day, eating crumpets in London." He savors the memory. "Yeah. Every night."

Rumi writes: "If the house of the world is dark, then love will find a way to make windows." Those transparent panes through which we see beyond what confines us, windows help us imagine something *más allá* our fears and crippling anxiety. Meister Eckhart suggests that we need to wipe clean the panes of our lantern, so that the light can be the strongest. We can imagine "crumpets."

There is a Tibetan saying that "where you have received the most love, that is home." But I think, LOVING is home. LOVING is nutritious. It feeds the grumbling stomach of our souls. We set ourselves up for disappointment and frustration if what we measure is receiving love. Our joy is in loving without regard for return. Then we see that loving IS our home. Once you know that, you'll never be homesick.

The homegirl Pooka, an African American gang member who has spent a lengthy amount of time in prison, is someone who, as we say in Spanish, *no tiene pelos en la lengua*. There are "no hairs on her tongue" to filter what she will say next. She hugs me the other day, and I'm wearing this aftershave that some señora from the parish gave me. When she releases me from her embrace, she says quite loudly, "What you got on? 'Bitch Be Gone'?" If you're fishing for a compliment with Pooka, you'll never know if you actually got one.

Famously, at a huge gathering in front of donors, she encouraged them to hire homies from our program. "We got skills like a muthafucka." They signed up in droves. What she also says often is: "At Homeboy, it's not about being all kumbaya. Love is our lens. It is how we see things."

It is not so much about "loving your enemies" but wearing a lens that helps you decide not to have any enemies. Nobody vs. Anybody. Love is wanting the well-being of others. We are always being invited to see with a different set of eyewear.

bell hooks writes that "without an ethic of love shaping the direction of our political visions and our radical aspirations, we are often seduced, in one way or another, into continued allegiance to systems of domination—imperialism, sexism, racism, classism." A great many of the mystics criticized the Church for losing track of the centrality of love, a failure that indeed seduced the Church to embrace empire and control as its centerpiece. We forgot to do love's work.

It will always be true that our proximity to the practice of love will be our only gauge of our progress. It is not our distance from hate that leads us forward, but our closeness to love. We aim to foster a habituated state that acknowledges the divine here and now. Then we choose to abide in that union.

A homie said to me once that he was just trying to "stay love-struck." Love IS, as they say, the undisputed heavyweight champion of the world. We then feel compelled to move through the world unclenched and upheld by tenderness. We ask ourselves each day, as Elizabeth Gilbert invites us: What would love have me do today? Emily Dickinson tells us that "Love—is anterior to Life / Posterior— to Death / Initial of Creation, and / The Exponent of Breath." An ethic of love shaping everything and setting all direction. Loving IS God, for God's sake.

I had a dream the night before a big funeral for Rita Chairez, a larger-than-life community activist in our parish of Dolores Mission and in all of Los Angeles. In my nearly forty years here, it was only the second time I can remember that we held the funeral outside in the plaza to accommodate the many people expected. I suppose I felt a high degree of pressure and anxiety, all self-imposed, as I was asked by the family to preside and preach.

So, Rita appeared to me in my dream. She told me, "We are all born. And we will all die. And all we have left is the tender time in between." I immediately turned my light on. My feet hit the floor and I wrote down her words, which became the core of my homily the next day.

My Jesuit brother Mark Torres, who has walked with folks at Homeboy for a quarter of a century, accompanied his mom through the agonizing years of Alzheimer's. She finished her life in a memory care facility, and by the end she no longer remembered anyone, not even her husband of sixty-three years. Mark went home to help his dad during this time and noticed that his father kept a folded piece of paper on the mantel of the fireplace, and he would put it in his pocket each day before heading out to visit his wife. The piece of paper had written on it these three letters, each with a period after it: "J. L. H." Mark asked his father what the letters meant. "Just. Love. Her.," his father said.

I like, nearly most of all, the punctuation. The emphasis is necessary when we just don't know where to turn. We are drawn to be bodhisattvas, pledging to imbue all with love and benefiting every sentient being. We are reminded to "stay lovestruck." It. Never. Fails.

Derek tells me there's a greeting in prison. He'll see a friend on the third tier and yell, "Hey, *cuate* . . . I send mines." And the response is always: "I send mines right back . . . full force." Sending yours is living one's life as God within us. It is a divinized life. My friend Jack Kornfield says that life is pretty much love and difficulty. In the end, only love matters. Love has the last word on who I am as a person. Love has the last word on who we are as a country and as a human race.

To be whole, we need to get our fears out of the way, to invite them in without judgment. Then fearlessness becomes the contour of our ultimate joy. *Mudita*, the Buddhist's notion of joy, is the vicarious delighting in another's well-being. Love as our true identity and deepest dignity. "I send mines."

It would seem that our choice in the world is either domination or love. Healthy people are able to love. Not good people. Whole people. Well people. When folks aren't healthy, they want to dominate. Van Gogh said, "The best way of knowing God is to love a great deal." It would seem certain that our prayer and meditation strengthen neural pathways. It helps us to love a great deal and to let go of control and power and the need to dominate. The homies who run Homeboy often say, "If it's a pattern, it's a problem." When folks color outside the lines, they say this. It sends them on the search for underlying thorns that present as "bad behavior." But by equal measure, if love is what we lead with, then that becomes a pattern. To greet each person with "I send mines" is a self-extension of generosity and outpouring of care for the other.

This is the kenotic path of Jesus. It is a self-emptying love that steps just outside my self-absorption. Less ego obsessed and more intentionally soulful. It acknowledges that any kind of clinging, but especially to the self, estranges us from the ground of our being. It connects us more and more with the mind of Christ, and our discovery is the freedom of our own authentic selves. With any luck, we find the unbroken awareness of the presence of God in every damn thing. Brother Lawrence calls it "practicing the presence of God." Like Shechinah in Jewish mysticism, it is this feminine presence of God imbued wherever we look. It transforms our lives from the inside out. It is how we can live in joy always. It's the only way we are able to say: "Right back at ya . . . full force."

Dollar Car Rental in Missoula, Montana, has pretty much run out of cars. I have with me Toby and Anthony, who are sitting off to the side as I negotiate the deal with the nice Dollar lady. She volunteers to walk me to the lone car in their lot, so I signal to the fellas to join us and bring their luggage. When the woman sees these guys, she stammers. Not because they were gang members, but because they were really, really large gang members. Let's just say that in the next few days, they'll eat their big-boned body weight in bison burgers and wash it down with huckleberry lemonade. She takes us to our car, and it's some impossibly mini vehicle. Every time we would subsequently walk to the car, Anthony would hum the Ringling Bros. circus song as we got in it. To this day, this tiny vehicle connects us when we are together, and we remind each other of the hilarious discomfort of it. Pope Francis speaks of the restlessness of love. It unsettles things and keeps us longing to break out of our tight squeezes.

I met Joey at Chico's funeral. He was inconsolable, sitting by himself in the foyer of Guerra & Gutierrez Mortuary. He knew Chico from this one park where they would get high together. When Chico was gunned down, the tragedy served to shake all the parts of Joey that were loose and untethered. I didn't know him, but his grief was large and drew attention to itself. We spoke and shared stories, and I gave him my card.

Joey showed up at Homeboy one day, and I tried to move him quickly through our process to begin the training program. Apart from a brief stint of rehab interrupting the middle of his eighteen-month program, he began to find an authentic self nestled in the middle of his loving spirit. I took him and another homie to Cleveland for some talks. When we drove up to LAX, neither had ever been there and had only seen the airport on TV. "I always wanted to see LAX in person. Imagine," Joey said, "from fuck-it list to bucket list."

Joey's healing involved great efforts to repair his relationship with his mom and siblings. There was a lot to overcome. He embraced "meek and humble" as his *modo de proceder*. He told me, finally, "I mean, I used to walk into rooms and everyone would say, 'Oh no. Here's Joey. Hide your shit.'" Then he added quietly, "But not no more."

Whole does not mean unbroken. It means welcoming and growing more and more at home with yourself. Joey later texted me out of the while blue yonder: "I promise I'm gonna give back to the whole world and continue the legacy of Homeboy." Buddhists might call this "right effort." All of life is a journey of love that ceaselessly installs windows. No one is completely whole or completely holy. It is all aspirational. The heart we work on is our own.

In some Christian circles, it is common to use this expression when talking about a beneficial presence with those on the margins: "We love on them." It always leaves me thinking, *Why wouldn't you just love them?* There is something distant and restrained in the expression. Perhaps it suggests loving from on high to those poor folks below. How love travels from the "saved" down to the "unsaved," perhaps. That maybe you love your family, but you "love on" everyone else. All of life is a journey of love, and if it is exquisitely mutual and totally reciprocal, there is no separation or distance. We love directly and head-on. No kumbaya and no need to hide your shit.

With the change of several laws, gang members who have been locked up for a long time finally "have action" and get released. One of those is Daniel, a senior citizen who spent twenty-six years in prison, with seventeen years of those in the SHU. He walks with a cane and a pronounced limp, having been shot in his youth. He has done a variety of things with us, along with "working on himself." Mainly he is something of a greeter at the "well"—the front reception desk. You have a sense with him that he is forever making up for lost time. He is playful, readily affectionate, and extremely well loved. His whole being seems to announce, "Life is too short not to enjoy it."

If I'm in my office and, say, talking to a homegirl, a coworker of Daniel's, he'll just stick his head in and whisper, pointing at the homegirl: "Don't get her mad." Or I'll be talking to a homie and again he'll pop in only to say, "Hey, G, is Memo bothering you?" Homies come in all the time and interrupt conversations in order to get a prayer or a blessing. This is nothing unusual. Again Daniel interrupts Memo, his great friend. "I need you to help me with a prayer right now." He bows his head, standing in front of my desk, with Memo sitting to one side. Daniel closes his eyes, leaning on his cane, and I extend my hand to do some sort of blessing prayer. When I'm done, Daniel opens his eyes, turns to look at Memo, and says, "Damn . . . he's still here," and limps out.

Once, he storms in and seems upset. "I don't know what's happening in the world. I mean, I was at church and down from me in the pew, a woman took out a cigarette and lit it . . . right there in church. I almost dropped my beer." He turns and walks out, barely giving me any time to register it all and laugh. The tender time in between, right before your eyes.

We are always being asked by life to find our courage to love what God loves and calibrate it to God's own heart. The roomier it is, the better. Simon steps into my office and he's rubbing his arm. He's a massive disruptor on most days. He starts fights and imagines homies looking at him with bad intent. I suppose he occasionally wanders into the category of "beyond the scope" of our ability to help him. And yet, the place persists with him. I've known him for several decades, and he was always a hothead. This temperament landed him in prison for quite a stretch, exacerbated by his endless fighting inside. Today he's rubbing his arm because "Sharon [our psych nurse] gave me an injection."

I ask, "Of what?"

"Vitriol," he says.

I tell him, "*Mijito de mi cora*, you got so much of that already. You don't need any more." He grabs his cell and looks it up to show me. It's Vivitrol, to help treat his opioid addiction. "In this ocean, in this sea," Rumi writes, "everything is allowed, everything fits." Even Simon. Beyond any injection to curb what plagues him is acknowledging this good, suffering soul as indeed precious. Then, in whatever time it takes, he not only feels seen; he believes his own preciousness.

Psychologist Albert Ellis points out that there are three errors in human thinking. First, when something negative happens, we ignore all the positive that surrounds it. Second, we don't just focus on the negative; we exaggerate it. We "awfulize" it. And finally, we tend to overgeneralize. We will say, "You NEVER," and "He ALWAYS," for example. I saw on a T-shirt in St. Louis: "Let's be better humans." I guess. Except if we see the positivity that surrounds the negative, we know that folks could not be one bit better. These "errors" in our thinking keep us from seeing the truth in each other. Letting love live through us is our truth.

A Sufi master, Hazrat Inayat Khan, writes: "God breaks the heart again and again and again . . . until it stays open." It is precisely this broken, wide-open heart that is able to fall into the immensity of the God of love. This is our ground. The ground is not the place you land on. It's more like the ocean you float in. An abyss of endless love, truly oceanic.

As I'm walking in New York City, I pass two construction workers. In a strong New York accent, one is describing the coffee he likes and therefore recommends: "Freshly . . . grounded . . . Turkish . . . cawfee." And in case anyone passing by missed his coffee preference, he repeats it loudly and with emphasis, "Freshly . . . grounded . . . Turkish . . . cawfee." And a mantra is born. I'm walking the streets of New York and breathing in the words: "freshly grounded." And this is all I want. To be freshly grounded in endless, oceanic love. Restored to a more grounded sense of myself in God's presence. This helps me sidestep "awfulizing" and keeps me mindful of what is wholly positive around me.

Stevie says wisely, "When you're grounded, then you can be an anchor for others." Finding the truth of the awakened heart, resting in God resting in me, anchored for you. No one is grounded once and for all. Every day, we need to be freshly grounded.

I read the obituaries every day in the *Los Angeles Times*. I note the year the deceased was born and think, *Wow. He's ten years younger than me*, or, *He's my age*. I can't help myself. I noticed one recently, featuring a bright, smiling face of a man in his forties. "Matthew Charles Slay of Trinidad, CA, passed away last week following a brief and courageous battle with an oversized piece of steak." I immediately thought it was a prank. Apparently, many readers felt the same. Matt's younger brother, Chris, wrote the obit, and it was whimsical and tender and filled with charming details about the life of his brother. Matt loved reptiles as a kid. Science fiction/fantasy was his thing. Chris didn't sugarcoat his brother's occasional brushes with the law. Affectionate and warm, the obit oddly galvanized the readers of the *LA Times*. A subsequent article was written about how it drew people in and together.

Matt choked on a piece of steak, and those with him performed the Heimlich maneuver to no avail. The paramedics arrived in ten minutes, but he went into cardiac arrest, and his brain was denied oxygen long enough that the family, finally, removed him from life support.

The obituary ends this way: "In lieu of flowers, please cut your food into bite-sized pieces and chew it thoroughly." A new mantra has arrived. I walk from my car to the office, bracing myself for the onslaught of hundreds and hundreds of gang members wanting my undivided attention. And I want to savor every breath that delights in them. So I breathe in the spirit that delights in my being, and I exhale in their direction. All the while, breathing in and out the mantra: "Chew thoroughly."

Love creates a circle wide enough to include everybody. It is why the most noble of all spiritual acts is the act of loving. Amie had written me years ago from Juvenile Hall: "I don't know what God sees in me." Amie has since made a discovery at Homeboy. "I realized that I wasn't entirely disposable." She explains that "what makes you a good gang member is that you don't care. I'm still stitching myself up in here. And fentanyl snatched my soul." Love grows when you practice it. Same with courage. Healthy people grow in both areas. Not moral people; healthy people. You begin to remember who you are. Then we can, as Mechthild writes, "clothe ourselves with ourselves."

After we sing "Happy Birthday" to Amie in our morning meeting, everyone chants "WE'RE GLAD YOU WERE BORN." She confides in me later: "There was a time I wished I wasn't born." We are all alone together. Fierce love brings us back to the entrance of our hearts. We can see clearly that our own stories matter. It can be this very broken heart that opens your loving heart. Love touches Amie's suffering, then the suffering turns love into mercy. The first letter of John does not say "Love God"; it says, "Love one another." The centrality of love says, "We're glad you were born."

So many of the folks at Homeboy are in recovery and will say, "One day at a time." I always tell them, "No . . . that's way too long." We need to cherish with every breath. Chew thoroughly. Hence, we connect cherishing with every breath we take, otherwise we forget. Would that the decision to love was a once-and-for-all thing. It isn't. Choosing to be in the world who God is . . . is not once and for all. We re-up with every cherishing breath we take. We want to find that undying fidelity to the quickening in our hearts. Our intention is that love always comes first. We know God when "we love a great deal." That's where the power is. And love always wants what God wants: the well-being of others.

"I hated myself for what I did," Joaquin confides. He's ten years into a fifty-year sentence when he finds himself overwhelmed with grief. He's in his cell alone, and tuning out some "Christian show" on the TV, until he aligns himself with this song being sung. He is filled with utter fullness, a quickening, that shifts him. He sobs and says from his very depth, "I'm sorry. I'm sorry. I'm sorry." What happens next is palpable and undeniable to him. He senses a fundamental lifting of things. "And all I felt was love. Everything left my body and I felt free. In an instant, I no longer believed in change 'out there,' but only 'in here,'" he said, patting his chest. Then he can declare: "I've been smiling ever since that moment."

Other inmates would express their annoyance. Joaquin would choose to brighten and say good morning to Oso, a grouchy *vato*, who "had all day." Oso would bark, "What's so good about it?" Joaquin would just point to the clouds, or the sun, or the sky. It was his decision to make windows with every cherishing breath. The ocean you float in.

This is the love that never dies. It allows even death to be put in its place as "not some annihilation but a culmination," as Jim Finley explains. It connects our first breath on earth with our last one. The culmination, our death, is, as Ram Dass suggests, "like taking off a tight shoe" at the end of the day. In loving, we practice death daily, freeing ourselves constantly from tight shoes.

Like a great many of my "dearly deporteds," Scrappy works at a call center in Mexicali. These homies, who came to this country when they were infants or children, got into a gang, went to prison, and now find themselves living in countries they don't know. They're bilingual, so they can handle that call from any English-speaking country. On our periodic Zooms, Scrappy tells our group about a woman who just unleashed a torrent of diatribe in his general direction. She unloaded on him. When she took a breath, he said, "Please, ma'am, you go right ahead. I will be your punching bag." Scrappy chooses to cherish with every breath. He wastes no time locking armor around his heart. He chews thoroughly, savoring it all. He does not want to get distracted in defensiveness. Nor does he want to exaggerate the negative. He does not want to forget to be kind.

Scrappy knows that you can't be curious and judgmental at the same time, so he chooses curiosity. Curiosity may well kill the cat, but it also neutralizes judgment. Scrappy's dedication to loving-kindness has become his highest expression of faith. He has found the radical humility to sustain it and the discipline to be alert to the other. Hope is not about how things turn out, but how we see things. Can we lean into them with curiosity and delight? Even with a woman screaming like a banshee? The gang on the Zoom expressed their admiration. "Damn, ma dawg . . . your goodness brings out my goodness." Scrappy didn't grow in goodness; he just sees it more clearly now.

Scrappy finds his joy in self-forgetting. He knows that dwelling on himself and his own "butt-hurtness" at being screamed at is its own punishment. He just won't have it. Gandhi says, "I must reduce myself to zero." This deported gang member knows how to let God be God in him. His own practice of contemplation and grounding gets unleashed in love, even for those who rip us a new one.

People sometimes speak of the "love of truth." Being loving, never stopping loving, loving being loving . . . this is the truth. Joel walked me to my car. It was his birthday. I wished him a happy one just as we all had sung in the morning.

"I'm getting old, G. More doctors' appointments than court appearances." We laughed. "You known me a long time, G . . . You remember. I used to make money. Now I make a living." He threw his arms around me. It took him a while to release me. And I recalled a line from a poem: "I'd follow love into extinction."

John of the Cross prays, "Burn whatever stands between me and union with the Beloved." Love doesn't allow "Us and Them." The truth of love is that it is the only way the distance between us as people gets burned away. Soon we find ourselves on this journey to union with love itself. A love that permeates you regardless of how things turn out. Then distance vanishes, just as homies want to see and be seen, as one homie put it, "with belonging eyes." It looks like this when you are "lovestruck."

"Pilgrimage to the place of the wise," Rumi writes, "is to find escape from the flame of separateness." The mystics of Islam describe

God as hidden by seven veils. The blindfold falls and we wipe clean the panes of the lantern; then being separate is no longer possible. Toro has spent more than half his life in prison. At forty-five years old, he comes into my office with a pronounced bounce and even giddiness. I don't know him, but he knows Homeboy. Gilbert, one of our security guards, encouraged him to walk through our doors. "Gilbert and me, we go way back like two flats on a Cadillac." Once Toro settles into a chair in front of my desk, he declares, "This place was built for me." You can feel distance vanishing. As we're winding down our time together, he points at the exuberance so clear in the reception area. "I see people smile," he says, taking in the scene outside my glass walls. He turns to me: "I want that smile." The veils no longer hiding much.

I ask Ramon if he's ever flown before. "I've seen *Con Air*." That counts. I tell him he'll have to share his story on this trip many times. He'll have to limit his remarks to five to seven minutes. He sits thinking a bit. "Five to seven minutes . . . in mosquito years it's a long damn time." To whatever amount of time you distill it, one's story will always be a "pilgrimage to the place of the wise." In this trek, trauma and transcendence touch the deathless nature of love.

At the start of the pandemic, my great friend Paul Lipscomb and I began meeting on Zoom and continued to meet once a month at 5:00 p.m. With our favorite amber adult beverage in hand, we hoist our glasses to each other and begin "cripesing." Paul, who had been a Jesuit, is now married to Lynne and has a daughter, Catherine. "Cripesing" comes from a time when an old Jesuit, presiding at mass, read the Gospel and, after he put it down, began his homily: "Cripes . . . that's a lot of theology." This always cracked us up. So, to this day, we "cripes" via Zoom, Paul in Portland and me in Los Angeles.

At the end of one of our "cripes" sessions, Paul mentions that he is rocking his forty-one-year-old daughter on his lap in a chair on the porch. Catherine is profoundly disabled and requires twenty-four-hour care. He has been rocking her in this chair for the entirety of her life. Typically, he sings some nonsensical ditty, and she screams gleefully. This night she's not having it. She bites her arm and throws the blanket over her head in defiance. Paul calculates where she is in the month. He rocks and rocks his "PMS-y daughter" and pauses, his words caught tight in his throat. "And I realize . . . that there is nothing missing here."

At this writing, three months from now, I'll be taking Glen and Cynthia of the lava cakes to London to help me address a huge youth conference. Finally, crumpets. I don't want to tell Glen that crumpets are basically Thomas' English muffins. But, like love, crumpets are aspirational, living in our mind's eye and connective to our longing. We find ourselves never homesick and, indeed, there is nothing missing here. "Everything is allowed. Everything fits." We find ourselves clothed with ourselves. It's precisely then that we can choose to follow love into extinction. One can't help but greet the world and say, "I send mines." I suspect nothing captures our entrance into full homecoming than when we learn that there IS nothing missing here. Love discovered as deathless.

8

THE HOUSEHOLD OF GOD

OVER HALF A CENTURY AGO, I WAS SITTING IN A CHAPEL AS A novice at the 5:00 p.m. mass. The older Jesuit priest had just proclaimed the Gospel where John the Baptist points out Jesus, who is walking nearby, to two of his disciples and says: "Behold, the Lamb of God." Then the celebrant began his homily: "John the Baptist points at Jesus and says, 'Behold the leg of lamb.'" He had my attention. I love lamb. Plus, in fairness to him, this mass was the only thing standing between us and dinner.

Then Jesus wants to know, as these two disciples of John trail him, "What are you looking for?" They say, "Where are you staying?" Our attention goes quickly to "Come and see," rather than spend much time on this odd question. They don't ask Jesus, "What's your philosophy?"; "What's the meaning of life?"; or "How do we get into heaven?" They long to know where he is staying. So they follow, and they stay.

Homies never say "stayed." They say "stood." "How late did you stay at the party?" "We stood all night," they'd say. In the Greek, "staying" is "abiding." It connotes something more than an Airbnb. It evokes more anchor than location. We went there and we stood.

Great outrage was directed toward the Los Angeles Dodgers when they wanted to honor the Sisters of Perpetual Indulgence on Pride Day for their considerable service and charitable works. A handful of Catholic groups, bishops, and dioceses shook their fists and proclaimed this nonprofit a "hate group" and "anti-Catholic." While doing their charity work, the "Sisters," all gay men, would also sometimes, somewhat, wear the mock wimples worn by nuns in 1954. Of course, this will only bother you if you want the Church to return to 1954. I know lots of nuns. They are secure enough in their ministerial presence in 2024 not to be too bothered by any of this. Richard Rohr says correctly that "only the false self is ever offended by anything." I suppose the same could be said of the Church. Once we are so thoroughly anchored in love, it will be hard to offend us.

We live in our perpetual distortions, highly defended and hugely fearful. Our defense of Catholicism can sometimes come at the expense of the Gospel. A national prelate said, "The Church must confront 'woke' social justice movements that aim to cancel Christian beliefs." This bishop sees these movements as "pseudoreligious replacements and rivals to traditional Christian beliefs." I'm not so sure they are. A movement to advance social justice is Gospel living, and it ought not be seen as a threat to the Catholic Church. A social justice movement doesn't cancel Christian beliefs but can complete and fulfill them. Where is Jesus staying? There is no threat here.

Gospel living is our very agency to present God's hope in the world. In Irish they don't say "the Word of God"; they say "the Verb of God." It is meant to be active. The Gospel of Luke is even more radical in this regard. It even sees kinship as a new economic arrangement. Luke really wants to upset the setup. The Verb of God. That isn't just some "social justice movement" or "pseudoreligious replacement," but, indeed, a new course, allowed to make its way through our culture, to shape the order of things: the kinship of God and a community of cherished belonging.

I don't say "Kingdom." The "King" keeps me from saying that. I don't say "Kin-dom" because it feels "dom." I say "kinship" because it's not a place but a stance. It's not a position; it's a disposition and a temperament. It is where we abide, an anchor. It's *acatamiento*.

A very prominent and wealthy Catholic was being honored for "promoting Catholic values." And I'm thinking, *Is that different from Gospel values?* And this article goes on further to say that this gentleman is praised for his "unwavering commitment to the Catholic Church." Again, isn't it supposed to be about the Gospel? The Church often strains itself in resuscitating the old and spends less time giving birth to the new. A return to "Latin and lace" rather than a more authentic following of Jesus. In the first letter of Peter, he tells us in Jesus we have been given "new birth to a living hope." "Make Catholicism Great Again" or "Live the Marrow of the Gospel"?

A Jesuit Nativity school flew the Black Lives Matter and Pride flags. They were told by the bishop to remove them. They refused because they believed the flags announced "the Good News to the poor." The Bishop withdrew their "Catholic" designation. I believe we should be careful of defending "Catholicism" at the expense of the Gospel. Are those two flags soaked with the Gospel? Yes. Inclusion, compassion, acceptance, and preferential care for "the widow, orphan, and stranger." Room in God's heart for everyone. The marrow of the

Gospel. These flags may well not be aligned with Catholic Church doctrine, but one couldn't make the case that they are foreign to the Gospel. They aren't.

We long, then, to be Gospel practitioners, not museum curators. Do we "keep the truth" or do we "preach the Gospel"? Do we live the "Good News to the poor," or do we merely re-create rituals from eighty years ago? We want to choose mystical activism. There have been countless Eucharistic Processions in every major city. A practice from eighty years ago. In front of Radio City Music Hall and in Times Square. I love the Eucharist. But organizers of these events say that these processions "transform the world by taking Jesus to the streets." On the contrary, Jesus' "streets" are not pavement in front Rockefeller Center, but, rather, the margins where folks carry more than they can bear. Go there. See Jesus. Be Jesus. This is where Jesus is "staying."

A lot of people seem to know that I like single-malt scotch. My preference is Laphroaig, a peaty, smoky taste that's not for everybody. The green bottle holds the scotch, but it is the scotch that is valuable, not the bottle. I'm a lifelong Catholic and will be until the day I die. But Catholicism is the bottle that holds the scotch. For me, it's the container where the Gospel should be held. Ross Douthat criticized Pope Francis in a *New York Times* opinion piece, lamenting that Francis will be remembered for having failed to teach the Catholic faith. Francis was too busy proclaiming the Gospel of Jesus.

For Catholics, the Catholic Church holds the faith but isn't the faith. Consequently, I never speak of "my Catholic faith" any more than I would the bottle holding the Laphroaig. I suspect doing so heightens our tribalism. The bottle just carries the thing of value. Through it all, perhaps we can agree with Rumi, who says that love is God's religion. Loving is how we practice it. I do this as a Catholic, but loving is the anchor.

We always need to be on the lookout for what I call the "Two Toots God." The God who couldn't give two toots about a wide variety of things that get, as the homies say, "our *chonies* in a knot." A sacred host that falls on the floor, an errant cuss word, following the marriage rite to the letter, the apostles grabbing grain on the Sabbath, or the Sisters of Perpetual Indulgence being honored at Dodger Stadium. God couldn't give two toots. We don't want to be a Church false enough to be offended. I'm equally certain that God gives a boatload of toots about 75,000 homeless people living on the streets of Los Angeles. Even so, God isn't displeased with our inaction, but adores us into feeling invited to do something about it. The marrow of the Gospel. Consequently, I suspect we are always greatly in need of some serious "toots alignment."

A Republican from Virginia blames nearly everything that plagues our society on our failure to follow God's rules for marriage. But the God we actually have is too busy cherishing us to have any time at all to care about the "rules." We endlessly keep score until we discover that our God doesn't.

I was channel surfing recently and found the Dalai Lama being interviewed. He seemed to be answering a question about the mark and measure of all "authentic religion." He ponders the question, repeats it in his labored English, then he places both hands over his heart, pauses, and says, "Warmheartedness." He mentions the word often in the course of the interview, like the word was a new discovery for him. The German word for "mercy" is "warmheartedness." This is the foremost passion of God, what Dylan Thomas calls "unjudging love." But, still, "warmheartedness" is a clunky word in English. Its clumsiness serves a purpose, though, and it gets even more clunky with the Dalai Lama's frequent use. "Warm . . . heart . . . ed . . . ness." Each time he says it, he gently places his hand over his heart.

He explains that there are two parts to this. There is the inner peace of it all and the discovery of our true selves in loving, AND we are propelled into the world to be "warmheartedness" there. Love is how we practice God's religion. It's like Saint Ignatius with *acatamiento*. We are not sent to the world to hide from it. We aren't meant to hoard and protect some mystical moment of inner peace. We are called to the world, yes, "to the streets," with affectionate awe and warm hearts. It's about choosing, all over again, with every breath we take, to be in the world who God is: compassionate loving-kindness. By letting love live through us, we ARE an "authentic religion" that is steady, true, and abundantly clear. You don't find the truth. You are found by it. Then you can live what James Finley calls a divinity-drenched life in a divinity-drenched world.

Gabriel is as purehearted as he is noble. He shows me the ticket for his court date and asks, "What month is six?"

I tell him, "June." I figure best not to tell him his entire court date is "6/6/6."

He and his lady bring their new baby into my office so I can bless him. "What's his name?"

"Jaden," Gabriel says.

I ask, "How'd you come up with that name?"

"Brainstormin' it."

"'Brainstorming'?"

"Yeah," Gabriel says, edging on the defensive. "I know lotsa words . . . 'hypothesis' . . . um . . . 'stereotype.'" Kicked my butt.

Gabriel can sometimes have his hair on fire. As a homie who

assiduously shaves his head, this is quite the accomplishment. I'm having a meeting with some senior homies when Gabriel storms in, greatly in need of a fire extinguisher aimed at his *cabeza*. He's as elliptical as ever. "The gas cards ... the vans ... empty." He's in too much of a hurry to bother with verbs.

A homie, Stevie, calmly looks at him and says, "Gabriel ... breathe with your ears."

In a quiet moment at the end of the day, you can sit with Gabriel, in all his simplicity and pure soul, and see him being found by the truth. "My parents didn't teach me how to live," he says, "but how to survive."

"The first job," Shirley Torres says, "is the inside job." You realize what Homeboy needs to be: a safe place where folks are seen and cherished. Where they can live, and not just survive. The first job. An abiding place, where "we stood all night." A divinity-drenched "household of God."

You greet the world with warmheartedness, and people believe they are good. The "household of God" reminds people of this fact rather than underscoring disappointment. The positivity of our warm hearts moves us forward and advances us toward a community of cherished belonging. The stumbling block is when we say, "There's good and bad in everyone." Negativity does not advance "evil" but just keeps us stuck in the place where we don't believe in our own goodness. Love makes progress. Fear and negativity keep us stuck in the mud.

When we recognize our world to be "divinity-drenched," it posits a hope that pulls us into the future. In 2010, I needed to lay off three hundred trainees because we had run out of money. When I broke the news to homie Smiley, he didn't say, "There goes my job," or "There goes that paycheck." He thought for a beat, then looked at me and said, "There goes my hope."

"Everything that's done," Martin Luther King said, "is done by hope." We often say about Homeboy, "Hope has an address." Most gang members can distill their woes, essentially, to a lethal absence of hope. If they can't conjure up hope, they are indeed stuck in the mud. Hope is a fundamental propellant that sends us forth, sufficiently, to keep us confidently humble as we move. At least we're moving. Carl Sandburg writes, "Hope is an echo, hope ties itself, yonder, yonder." We can breathe a sigh of relief as long as there is a "yonder."

The prophet Isaiah speaks of "a just savior . . . meek and riding on an ass." First of all, this reminds me of a talk I gave somewhere in Georgia, when I described a homie as having "a loud-ass voice." A woman came up to me afterward, incensed that I said "ass." I told her that Jesus rode on one. Let's just say I didn't win the argument. But when Jesus says "meek and humble of heart," these are not two qualities among a list of qualities. These seem to be a passageway to something quite large and spacious. Humble and meek ushers in this essential disposition as Church. It maintains an actual emptiness that God reliably fills. For when we're empty, our mystical voice shows up and, like God, we have room for everybody.

On a flight not too long ago, I was returning to my seat from the restroom. Someone on an aisle seat has a book resting on their tray table, and I can see the distinctive turquoise cover of my book *The Whole Language*. I think, *Wow. Someone's reading my book*, so I approach, *lo prifas*, only to discover a man slouched in his chair, snoring loudly. I believe he might have been drooling. Apparently, reading my books is the next best thing to a CPAP machine. I tell one of the homies traveling with me and he starts to get up. He wants to take a picture of him. Humiliation is my compass. But, truly, meek and humble always creates a thoroughfare to something more expansive.

Always. The mystical voice whispering in your ear to have a light grasp, never offended. Breathe with your ears. Too busy loving.

I am speaking at a fundraiser in Fresno for a partner organization of our Global Homeboy Network. The evening grows too late for me, and I depart to my room in the hotel where the event was held. I leave the two homies behind to carry on the mingling duties. I'm bleary-eyed as I swipe my key at my door and the stubborn lock is all red lights. I try multiple times. Finally, I trek down to the registration desk and explain my dilemma. "No problem, Mr. Boyle, here's a new key." I head to the eighth floor again, try the key, same red light. The elevator returns me to the nice lady at the desk. "I'm so sorry, Mr. Boyle. You go back up there and I'll send a maintenance man now."

It doesn't take long, and the guy finds me posted at my door. He has a toolbox and a handyman's belt slung at his waist with hammer and screwdrivers and such. He doesn't need all this stuff and quickly retrieves a card that, I guess, opens every room.

The screaming doesn't begin immediately. There are several beats, when from inside the room the two of us can see a middle-aged woman, in a bathrobe, a towel swirled over her head, illuminated only by the TV as she sits at the edge of the bed, watching the tube.

Then she screams. I can only think: *Why is this woman in my room?* At that exact moment, I realize that my room just might be across the hall. I pivot, place my card on the other door, and the green light gives me passage. I immediately go searching for that shovel to dig the hole necessary to bury myself in. Humiliation as my compass. The mystical whispering voice reliably freeing me to grasp lightly. Yonder. Yonder.

In the early years, Christianity was a subversive spiritual movement of equality, emancipation, and peace. I suppose, a "woke" social justice movement. It was a way of life, not a set of beliefs. It got famously co-opted when Constantine became emperor in the early fourth century and the mission took a decided back seat, as loyalty to the Institution became the dominant strain. Mechthild criticized the Church for not being anchored in love. She thought if we just lived by love, we wouldn't have to say very much. We try not to be seduced by domination and empire control and wish to return to the orthodoxy of love. Consequently, we need all the voices in the room we can gather, otherwise we just settle for power and control. We need the flags announcing "Pride" and "Black Lives Matter." We need women demanding their place. We are always in need of a spiritual bypass redirecting blood around our blocked arteries. Perhaps it's time to recycle Christianity, as Brian McClaren suggests. Redeemed and reconsecrated, moving from our entrenched dualism to some glorious sense of interbeing. This way of life points the way. Ephesians says, "Then you are no longer strangers and aliens . . . but members of the household of God."

Disciples must always look for alignment and resemblance. Pope Francis gives Communion to Nancy Pelosi, as an act aligned with the heart of God and resembling the compassion of Jesus. Yet people are offended. I'm at the Atlanta Convention Center, waiting to speak. When I hear a bishop ask the crowd, "What makes a good Catholic?" I realize, sitting there, that I could, well, give two toots. I feel this about the question itself as well as about the answer he ends up giving. It all seems miles away from alignment and resemblance. So distant from mystical activism and Gospel practice. Far from where Jesus is staying.

The Acts of the Apostles speak about "belonging to the way." I recognize that this is my longing. I want to be accused of belonging to the way. In our movement toward a cherishing community, we can witness the transformation from folks at the margins feeling, perhaps, tolerated, but then invited. Before long, they see they are being offered inclusion. But the final resting moment comes in belonging. There is alignment and resemblance to the marrow of the Gospel in belonging. We don't just belong to the way; belonging *is* the way.

A recent study underscored the correlation between the number of worlds you belong to and the number of colds you get. "Worlds" here means things like coaching Little League, work, church, cycling, stamp collecting. The more worlds . . . the fewer colds. Homegirl Catalina told me, "When I stepped through those doors the first time, I was so nervous. But the first face I saw was Largo's [Alvin, a smiling homie in a wheelchair, who would sign folks in] . . . It was then that I knew I was in the right place." "Worlds" are our infinitely diverse "right places." They keep us healthy.

I'm cooking dinner for all the Jesuit novices at our house, feeding about twenty people. I'm checking on the chicken and constantly stirring the polenta. I'm not a big fan of "cheerleaders" in the kitchen while I cook. I like my Zen solitude while I stir polenta. Oh, well . . . there are five novices hovering. One of them says, "Can I ask you a question?"

"Sure," I say, not one bit happy to be questioned.

"How do you talk to people about faith?"

"I don't," I say, as I tend to the burbling polenta. All five novices gasp. Audibly. I'm startled by their intake of air. I reduce to simmer. "I don't. Faith can just sometimes stay in our head and be about beliefs and doctrine. Once in a while, it moves to your heart. But our faith has to make its way to our feet. It's not about yakkin'. It's about feet standing in the right place, walking in the right direction." Increasing the "right places."

A week before this novice asked me that question, my friend Bishop David O'Connell was gunned down in his home. He was much on my mind as I spoke of the importance of feet. I had seen Dave a week before he was killed and he always "chose to brighten" when he greeted you. He pulled the favor right out of you, and you felt favorable when the encounter was done. He was proof that health, wholeness, and holiness are all interchangeable. He was a Gospel practitioner and mystical activist. To be connected to the God of love is to know flourishing joy and fearlessness. These are the marks of authentic discipleship and also the measure of holiness and health. Faith finding its way to your shoes. The Household of God is filled with folks who stand at the margins so that the margins get erased and we can walk each other home to holiness. We stood all night. Filled with warmheartedness and offended by nothing human.

There was a time in the Church when our very humanity was seen as an impediment to a relationship with God. Now we see it as a requirement. I'm waiting for Javi to show up so I can bring up the issue of his increasing pugnaciousness at our headquarters. I'm hoping to keep him off our "no-fly list" that would temporarily bar him from entering the office. Our security guards have about had it with him. Today he arrives an hour late for work, which does not help his case. I flag him in.

"Why are you late?"

"Oh," he says, "I had to go to the CVS, then drop my grandma off at detox." I think to myself, *Okay, you just won the prize today for "Sentences I've never heard before."*

"*Mijito*, why do you get in so many fights?"

He pleads with me: "Come on, Pops, it's summer." (Now, you tell me, what do you say to that?) And yet, nothing human is "outside the tent." As Rumi writes: "In this ocean, in this sea—everything is allowed—everything fits." We all just want to avoid the "no-fly list."

I took a vanload of homies to the Universal Amphitheater for an Extravaganza Christmas show. We got free tickets and sort of VIP backstage passes. It was as an elaborate affair, as you could imagine. It had the Rockettes from Radio City Music Hall, singers, acrobats, and appearances from Santa to Jesus. The manger scene included a menagerie of varied animals who were surely not present when Mary gave birth, unless Ringling Bros. followed that star, too. One of our troop, Fili, who was in a wheelchair, having been paralyzed many years before in a gang-related shooting, was by my side during the backstage part. On occasion, the sight of someone in a wheelchair can activate some infantilizing tendency. A woman, seemingly in charge, came over to Fili and spoke to him like he was a child. Surely she meant well, but the patronizing irritated Fili a bit. The woman leaned down to him: "Would you like to pet the camels? Let me see what I can do." She walked away.

Fili looked at me and grumbled, "I'd rather pet the Rockettes."

Nothing human need be feared, discarded, or disparaged. God just wants to be revealed in it all. No need to narrow how God communicates.

Bill Cain has written that the font of revelation is not closed but close. God did not stop speaking at the end of the Bible. God is still speaking . . . in Bishop Dave, in Esperanza, in Javi, in the Beloved present in every kindness and gentle moment. A homie, Douglas, writes me from prison: "I'm taking this biology class. Yeah, I go to school . . . go figure. Back in 1668, there was an Italian physician and he had this theory [spontaneous generation]. He thought that life could just spontaneously appear. This is outdated. It got disproven by Louis Pasteur in 1859. People used to think the world was flat, a long time ago. Turns out, it's round. People's way of thinking changes over time. I'm trying to change." Revelation is close, not closed. Why would Douglas, whom I've known for a long time, write me this? I suppose he wanted to assert that some notion of himself was also "outdated." His world is round now, not flat. He knows that his goodness cannot be canceled—knocked out of the ring—by any past horrific action on his part. Now "disproven," he can grow in love, not goodness. Humanity is a requirement.

I suppose I prefer to say "disciple" rather than "Christian." A disciple grows in love, not goodness, since the goodness is there, unshakable and awaiting fuller discovery. Religion by nature is legalistic, but God isn't. Disciples know this in the depth of their soul. True disciples don't live God-fearing lives, but God-seeing lives. In an age of cable news advocating loathing and fear, people of the Gospel have to be about loving and fearlessness. God is compassion in everything. Gandhi decided to be a disciple of Jesus and never stopped being a Hindu. Safe to say, he was a faithful disciple. As disciples, we don't want healing to be deferred. Now is the time. Here is the place. These are the people with whom you can walk. At Homeboy, a staging area of Church, it is precisely this culture of kindness, this soft place for hard conversation, that stimulates the body and soul to heal itself. We see wholeness, and it helps us all to rewire—not just the traumatized, but every one of us. Since we are all walking wounded, only tenderness is mutually transformational. This is what leads to awakened hearts.

On my recent visit to an Anglican Maori boarding school for boys, Te Aute College in New Zealand, Rachel, the first woman principal in 175 years, told me, "The students come here for healing. Why would we waste our time just educating them?" We rewire by way of an exquisitely mutual commitment to relational wholeness. The Maori archbishop John Don Tamihere (one of the greatest men I know) speaks of *kaupapa*, which suggests that "if you hold up a high purpose, people unify." Staging areas of Church, soaked in kindness, find a larger love and higher purpose. Unity is the byproduct.

Jesus says, "Don't let your hearts become drowsy." He could have said "eyes" or "speech" or "mind." He says "hearts." How do we keep vigilant hearts, not because death is coming, but because life is happening in all the wild contours of the human condition? How do we get beyond the brutalities of our minds that keep our hearts drowsy? We need attentive hearts to make way for a universal, all-inclusive belonging. We need to step away from a Christianity that supports exclusion and superiority. It's a head scratcher that so many Christians are frightened and rebuke the notion of "woke" when the entirety of Advent is about waking up. In Mark 13 alone, Jesus says it six times.

Famously, the Buddha, the Awakened One, is on the road and demonstrably happy, wearing a saffron robe. A man sees him and asks: "Are you a god?"

"No," the Buddha says.

"Are you a magician?"

"No."

"Are you a man?"

"No."

"What are you, then?"

And the Buddha says, "I am awake."

I ask a homie to attend a meeting for me and then report back. He walks into my office later and I ask how it went. "It could have been a car show," he says, "People tooting their own horns." Meek and humble is us at our most awakened. If I keep it from being about me, then it allows for inclusion and keeps a dominating superiority from taking over. *Kaupapa.*

At Homeboy, I'm often cautioning our senior staff to be allergic to "NO." It can be painful for our folks who are at the very end of their rope to hear "No." The Department of Motor Vehicles says "No." The Church can't be "Dr. No," too. Our quest is this: How can we get to "Yes"? We think "No" is strong and principled and "Yes" is a pushover. We're convinced "No," like Wonder Bread, builds character twelve ways. Getting to "Yes," however, pulls folks in and supplies a combo burger of help and hope, where everyone gives a dose of assistance.

A woman, Cynthia, mother of five, living in her car, is weighed down by a universe of intractable dilemmas with a side order of catastrophes. I give her some money, send her down to the Jesuit volunteer in charge of Pampers, and then have her talk to Pooka, in charge of housing. Before she leaves, she drops by my office in tears. I thought she was crying because so many of her issues remained still unattended. I was wrong. She was grateful for all the yeses she received. Augusto "Goose" Dolce, the founder of God's Pantry, says to the staff who come to him with a query: "The answer is yes. Now . . . what's the question?"

Brendan Busse, the pastor of Dolores Mission and superior of my Jesuit community, tells us at dinner about a woman who sent him an email.

The woman's young daughter asks her, "Hey, Mom, why are we now going to Dolores Mission and not that other church anymore?"

The mom says, "Well, at that other church, the priest was afraid, and he wanted us to be afraid, too."

The daughter ponders this and says, "So, at Dolores Mission, they don't make us afraid . . . they make us brave?"

We recognize that we are the Church and the mark and measure of our authenticity as disciples will present as joy and fearlessness. Its opposite is sadness and fear. We choose, then, to become a Church where your heart skips a beat with joy instead of missing a beat with fear. Unafraid of the Sisters of Perpetual Indulgence.

Saint Thérèse of Lisieux said, "My vocation is to love." Fear can't muster up compassion—only love can do this. The soul of Jesus is always telling us, "Don't waste your heart on fear." We can't wait for the Institutional Church to find its bravery. The people of God need to move forward. There is no bravery in returning to 1954. If we wait, cobwebs grow on our hearts. They get drowsy. If we keep moving, bravely . . . cobwebs don't stand a chance. It begs the question: What would we do as the Church if we weren't afraid or offended by anything?

On our way to Cleveland, Southwest Airlines gives us a layover in Las Vegas. I tell the homie couple traveling with me, Ivy and Jesse, "If you need me, I'll be playing Wheel of Fortune." They roll their eyes and shake their heads. I can't tell if they're horrified or not.

Jesse comes back later and surreptitiously takes a picture of me at the Wheel slot machine. He sends it to me and says, "I may need this for blackmail purposes."

Twenty minutes later, I find them at the gate and I hand each one hundred dollars in twenties. "Yeah . . . you talk shit about the Wheel of Fortune."

"Damn," Jesse says, "You won this . . . on the Wheel of Fortune?"

"Forty dollars of it," I tell him. "The rest I won . . . at that Wells Fargo ATM over there." The heart wants us to skip a beat in joy.

Joy and fearlessness are the marks and measure of the Church we long for . . . the household of God. Church as museum is sometimes what we think might be the only choice left us. The great Brian Mc-Claren says so helpfully, "I don't have to choose between staying Christian compliantly or leaving Christianity defiantly. I can stay defiantly." He calls this "Occupy Christianity." Dissent is renewal in time of religious stagnation, pious clichés, clericalism, and mind-numbing habitual practices. We stay defiantly by finding the invitation, always asking the question of the Church: To what ought we to give our hearts? We always seem to know what the Church is against. John Paul II was against a "culture of death." Benedict was against a "dictatorship of relativism." Of course, relativism seemed to be the operating policy of Jesus, who had such a reverence for complexity. Francis proposes a "culture of encounter," a clear invitation to relational wholeness. It is this positioning that leads to kinship, Nobody vs. Anybody. We can occupy Christianity from this place and stance.

We were on the shuttle to get us to our rental car at the Albuquerque airport. Mutt and Jeff were with me. Hector, a "Jeff" tiny guy, and Anthony, a much bigger "Mutt" *vato*. The recorded voice on the shuttle says: "Welcome to the Land of Enchantment."

Hector brightens. "You didn't tell us we were coming to the Land of Enchantment." I can't tell if he's yanking my chain or greatly anticipating some enchantment. By the fifth time the recorded guy says it, Hector says loudly, "Yeah, yeah, Land of Enchantment . . . Prove it."

Whenever I'd get up to leave, anywhere—at the airport, at the hotel, at a restaurant, to go to the restroom—anytime I stepped away, Hector would say again, loudly, "Be safe. Make good choices." Our first morning of the trip, they have a huge breakfast in the hotel. That night we meet about ten folks, friends and sponsors of our trip, for dinner, and a woman is asking Hector where we had lunch. He tells her that we didn't stop for lunch.

"You didn't have lunch?" she asks.

Hector turns and looks at me with puppy-dog eyes, and says to her, "Child abuse."

They gave, several times, their "seven minute" story. Once, Anthony returned to his seat, *desanimado*, lamenting that his talk was only five minutes this time. Hector mock chided him, "Fool . . . THEY PAID FOR SEVEN MINUTES."

Our big talk is to follow the Sunday mass, which we attend. Hector asks me why the kids all left before the readings. I tell him so that the kids can attend the liturgy of the word at their level. Hector asks if he and Anthony should go with them. Hector is as short as the kids, but he's thirty-seven years old. I am impressed that he knows all the responses at mass. Later, he tells me how surprised he was himself. "I couldn't believe I still knew the Apollo's Creed."

The priest means well, but the homily drones on for twenty-five minutes, which I believe may well be ministerial malpractice. Not as bad as a surgeon amputating the wrong leg, but still. A man walks out in the middle of it, shaking his head with what appears to be disgust. Not everyone is a good homilist. But everyone owns a watch. Anthony and Hector, God love 'em, sit through it and find grace and marvel with an "all the disciples in one place" kinda vibe. God love 'em. It humbles me to see their unmitigated acceptance of such a long-winded homily. They taught me "to breathe with my ears."

The marrow of the Gospel is essential. But what is essential never imposes itself on us. Consequently, we find ourselves bombarded by the nonessential, which always seems to make its case. The Maori hold out the notion of *Oranga Ake*, which is an ever-increasing life or flourishing. Their sense of church is to weave people together like a basket, fortified by tying loose strands to find their strength in the larger love and higher purpose. It is this that unifies.

The disciples snap off the grains to eat on a Sabbath, and Jesus faces the adamance of the categorical. His hope is to replace it with a reverence for complexity and an honoring of the higher purpose. The fearful reside in the categorical. The room they stay locked in is that of our binary adamance. The invitation is to move beyond mere ideology and dualistic thinking. We strive for a nondual way of seeing, anchored in the compassion of God. Maybe we free up our grip on the notion of "free will" and usher in some compassion. Perhaps we can begin to celebrate life more, rather than judge it.

The ultimate goal for the Buddhist is to realize your true Buddha nature and live in enlightened compassion. We all have a deep mystical sense that Jesus wants the very same thing. We can spend great energy admonishing religious institutions for clinging to doctrine that is wildly out of step with our contemporary reality. But it is not about keeping up with the times. The goal is not to be contemporary, but radical. We don't want to be out of step with the God of love who endlessly invites us to create a household of enlightened compassion. Waking up happens in community.

The "spreads" crisis of 2003 taught me a lot about such a household. "Spreads" are awful jailhouse concoctions meant to feed many. A clean garbage bag is filled with Vienna sausage, Cheez Whiz, pickles, all manner of hot sauce, sardines, Flamin' Hot Cheetos, and a million other random food items, all surrounded with a sizable nest of ramen that takes a bath in boiling water and, after a time of rest, is served to the incarcerated masses. This time-honored tradition found its way to Homeboy.

Every day the homies would arrive, someone would collect a

dollar from those who wanted to participate in the feast, and a group would go down to the dollar store and fill the order of edible crap. The foraging committee would return and then take over our small kitchen and begin to toss everything together. The care and feeding of the plastic bag would nearly take folks to noon, when plastic bowls would get filled and people fed. Exactly no work got done otherwise in the office.

The "spreads crisis" was brought to one of our senior staff meetings, where the general consensus recommended that this daily ritual should end. The adamance of the categorical. Grumbling ensued. Finally, Father Mark pleaded his case. He insisted that an activity like the daily spread enhanced our beloved community and symbolized the very nature of the heart of God. There is room for every imaginable food item just as surely as there is space in God's own heart for all of us. The spreads continued. The homies hoisted Mark on their shoulders. Though the spreads grew less frequent, they remained a rich symbol of everyone being fed from a single source, comprising the oddest ingredients. The great delusion is separateness, and the call and invitation is to unity. Divinity drenched.

During Pride Month, I walked past Southwest Airlines Gate 25 at LAX. The gate was brightly festooned with sparkly streamers and balloons, all in the colors of the Pride flag. Hanging high above the gate agent's desk were the words "Everyone Welcome." I stopped in front of it and I thought, *Please tell me the Church is at least as inclusive as Southwest Gate 25.*

Fearlessness is the doorway to joy, and our hearts can skip a beat anew as we see that "everything fits." God only wants the circle to widen, and that's our communal task in the Household of God. The armor around our hearts clanks to the floor when, with great humility, we ask at every turn, "Where are you staying?" More anchor than location. Disciples rest here in God's love and live out of that anchored place. The flourishing temperament we embrace wants to abide in the marrow of the Gospel. No time for things that God could give two toots about. We all want to be invited to the highest purpose held up to us. We will unify if it's held up. Offended by nothing. Everyone welcome. Drenched in divinity.

9

THE FASTEST ROUTE

I'VE JUST FINISHED MY PART OF THE GRAVESIDE SERVICE. NOW it's time for the doves—my cue to exit. I never stay for the doves. Maybe it's the treacly theology preached by the dove handler. Anyway, as I make my "Irish exit" and as I walk to my car, I see three older homies that I've known for forty years, since they were quite young. Homies always situate themselves at the very edges of these services. They stand by the road, at quite a distance from the gathered mourners and the dove wrangler, still explaining the symbolic meaning of it all. I join these three and chat a bit before taking my leave.

We reminisce about the time one of the homies from the Pico Gardens housing projects wanted to save money on the "dove part" of the service. He and another homie corralled a bunch of project pigeons into a huge, ungainly box, with air holes punched in it and loosely taped, drove it to the cemetery, and, at the appointed moment, opened it. Some of the angry birds literally flew into a rage and thought every woman there was Tippi Hedren from Alfred Hitchcock's *The Birds* and started beelining for their hair. Others just hopped out of the box and wandered serenely around. Still others stayed in the box, liking it fine there. We stifle our laughs as we all recall that day.

I turn to leave and see something. I nudge the homie next to me and he passes the nudge to the next homie and so on. Soon, all four of us are staring at the same thing. We are silent. Across the road from us, atop a short hill, is what appears to be a tattooed gang member, in a graduation cap and gown, all alone, taking a selfie in front of the wall of a mausoleum. He then slowly kneels in front of the wall and gently weeps, pressing his hands over his eyes. We are still, until one of the homies says, "I got chills right now."

"Fuck," says another, "I'm crying." Soon we all are.

After a tiny space of time, I ask, "What's your best guess?"

"He's visiting his mom," says one.

"Yeah, definitely . . . his *jefita*," adds another. We are wrapped in some unifying cloak that joins us to each other and to the stranger on the hill. We find our point of connection as members of the human family. We discover the sanctity of interconnectedness. This is the deathless presence of Jesus. Hafiz writes: "I have come into the world to see this: the sword drop from men's hands even at the height of their arc of rage because we have finally realized there is just one flesh we can wound."

The unifying cloak is the assertion that there is no separation between God and Us, and Us and each other. At Homeboy we experience this "milieu therapy" where we are constantly reminded of our inter-abiding, mutual indwelling, profound kinship with each other. A cherishing love brings us to that. Acts of the Apostles tells us, "God makes no distinction between us and them." Sergio says of this line: "That's what heaven tastes like." Indeed, it is the nature of love to flow from gathered mourners to grizzled homies to a lone gang member sobbing on a hill in his cap and gown. Arundhati Roy writes: "Another world is not only possible, she is on her way. On a quiet day, I can hear her breathing."

George was trying to explain the "secret sauce" of Homeboy to a couple who dropped by for a tour of our headquarters. He walked them through the reception area and wanted to describe "that certain something" this place held for him. "I don't know how to put it," he began, "but this place . . . has an aroma." True enough. It smells like belonging. And, yes, it tastes like heaven.

A homegirl, Alicia, from Las Vegas, after getting her first tattoo removal treatment with us, wrote me a heartfelt letter expressing her gratitude. "I'm inspired by the air in the place. I felt belongance."

Part of what Alicia and George were showcasing was the fact that intention is the most powerful ability that human beings have. The aroma was people deciding to be tender, even given their acrimonious tension with each other as gang rivals. We arrive at the clear intention to be tender, and it catapults us out of our default mode—self-absorption—and it lands us in the lap of belonging. Along the way, sturdiness and an emotional strength replace a hypersensitivity to anxiety. We give each of us the power and permission to contain everything with kindness, to find a balance and recalibrate and hold even our "panicked story lines," as my friend Pema Chödrön puts it. Intending only to be anchored in gentle cherishing. Kindness becoming atmospheric. Kinship as a frequency.

Half the members of "the Council" are homies who have gone through our program and now run Homeboy Industries. We gather three mornings a week to take the temperature of the place and perhaps mention some trainees who might be struggling. At one juncture, José turns to me and says, "Someone said once, 'Two peas are better than one.'"

There's a pause. I say to him, "Son, no one . . . has ever said that before." After yet another pause, we all melt with laughter. Then we excavate. "Two peas in a pod" meets "Two heads are better than one." The secret sauce may well be that we are all in this pod together and anything of significance rarely happens alone. May we continually see the world to come in this one. A unifying cloak draped over us all.

Certainly, gang members walk through our doors encased in the defended self. They seek a place that is safe, and though they might be hard-pressed to say further, they also hope to be seen, and then, indeed, cherished, as the finishing touch. Belonging creates and undoes us both. We are all allowed, initially, to stand in the ruin of ourselves. It is safe to do so. This issues in a healing that leads to a sturdy resilience, and folks leave here nearly thriving and flourishing.

Sharky can chart the exact years. "From age five to twelve. Yup, five to twelve." During these seven years, his father was lost in a crazed concoction of cocaine and PCP use, rendering him tirelessly paranoid and unpredictably violent. Restraining orders and police were all powerless against his father's skulking and threats. Sharky's family would move. His father would find them. He would confront little Sharky on the street and accuse his mom of sleeping with every man in accusing distance. "I'm going to kill her. Then kill you and then blow my brains out." Seven years. Sharky would confide and cry in his mother's arms, and she'd hold him and rock him and allow him to cry all he wanted. "And I mainly remember her heartbeat. It consoled me."

Sharky retrieved this image again, after years of gang involvement, incarceration, and very heavy drug use himself. "I walked into Home-boy, finally, and there it was. I could feel it the second I walked in. The heartbeat. It's there. Just like I remembered it." He pauses to find his footing. "Yeah, it's the heartbeat of God."

A great many gang-intervention programs seek to have "credible messengers" who, because they've lived the gang life, the thinking goes, will be the more suitable communicators to younger gang mem-bers, so that these young ones . . . will make better choices. Though all credible messengers are gang members of color, it still is an idea born from the outsider view. Folks looking in and saying that gang mem-bers are the appropriate messengers. Certainly, at Homeboy, the ma-jority of our senior staff are homies and homegirls. But that's about ownership, not message. Who can cherish? Anyone with a pulse. If it's about advice, maybe just gang members. But it's not about mes-sage and certainly not about advice, but, rather, loving, caring folks who pay attention and choose to be the very notice and heartbeat of God. We don't want to settle for understanding gang members; we want to hold out for believing in them.

"Provocative" is Monique's middle name. I suspect that the brutal treatment she received as a young girl growing up in Boyle Heights and the multiple head injuries she endured were the roots of her fly-ing off. Beginning at six years of age, she was repeatedly molested by her stepfather. She was napping next to her younger brother. Next thing she knew, there was the heavy weight of her stepfather on top of her. He held his hand tightly over her mouth. "I feel like that hand has been held over my mouth since then," she says. After her stepfa-ther got off of her, "all I worried about was my brother lying next to me. I just wanted him to be safe." This sexual abuse continued for another seven years.

Monique is proof that, with trauma, our executive function shuts down. Fear sets in and is displayed for all to see as contempt for anyone who sidesteps her. Monique is the face of unprocessed fear, hurt, and shame. She would lose it daily and get in the face of rivals whom she thought were looking at her "sideways." One day I called her in and chewed her out a bit about some moment of wild provocation. My correction of her wasn't loud, or shaming, or less than clear. Still, her defensiveness was maintained at its highest register.

The next morning I texted her, "Thank you for listening to me yesterday." Of course, there was no evidence that she had. She texted back with a picture of her, in our reception area, sitting and holding, quite tenderly, someone's infant. She writes: "Homeboy is where your heart becomes soft." We are less interested in offering "wraparound services" than we are in creating a wraparound place. We want to hold Monique with a tenderness no different from the gentle embrace of this infant. It is precisely from this location that we know that we don't have enemies; we have injuries. That we don't have hate; we have wounds. And, really, we don't have fear. We only have the shared ruin of our common, human brokenness.

When Steve Avalos encounters a homie who manipulates, he calls him a "shenanigizer." Mark Torres and I have a private nickname for a homie named Fidel, who came to us straight out of prison. I think I knew him from juvie and early camp days. I hire him on the spot, but a week later he disappears. One solid week, no call, no show. When he stumbles, exhausted, into my office, a week after that, he tells me he was holed up in a "mo mo" with several females and alcohol and drugs. When he was sated, he came back and said: "That's it for me. No more shenanigans." Mark and I still call him "Shenanigans."

A place that welcomes you to safety has room to allow standing in the ruin of your life until you are able to inhabit the healthier place. "No more shenanigans" is not about deprivation and a full embrace of morality. It is, rather, a reservoir of joy never before experienced. A culture of encounter. It's not about a message, so it's not about a messenger. Atmospheric cherishing. A frequency of tenderness. All invitation and not a trace of indictment.

I found myself saying the other day to one of the senior staff, "What's the point of healing, if it doesn't lead to a community of cherished belonging?" I ask myself: *If we allow people to live in tents on Main Street, are we honoring their civil rights, or are we ignoring that they belong to us?* The poet William Stafford writes: "Your job is to find out what the world is trying to be." Creating this community is our job beyond one's individual healing. Our imagination wants us to see the Beloved community as when the "WE" in "We the People" is not just some of us but, indeed, all of us.

Saint Basil the Great was thirty years old when he experienced an intense conversion. He said it was like "waking from a profound sleep." Consequently, he wanted to devote his life to God and went touring many monasteries. He eventually started one himself in Caesarea. His emphasis was not on an individual's asceticism, but rather on creating a place that celebrated community. Equally, Homeboy is a space for an individual not just to heal, but to break forth into the formation of some new collective living. Basil's place was hugely inclusive. People were welcomed, and the monastery had a school and an orphanage and met the needs of the poor.

Homeboy, like Basil, wants to present something to the world. "What the world is trying to be." Not some ideal that can't be attained, but the front porch of the house everyone wants to live in. A homie told me he joined a gang at fourteen. "That's when I stepped off the porch." You present the "porch" again and hold it out for people to see and to catch a whiff of the aroma.

We want to live in this house. A bakery where enemies who used to shoot at each other make croissants side by side. "You know what the best part of Homeboy is?" a homie tells me. "The HOME part." A place that's more home than home. A sanctuary where deeply traumatized people can find their true selves in loving. A petri dish where nonjudgmental and compassionate acceptance grows into a contagion. Yes, "HOME" happens here, but home does not just happen. We have to see it with intention and fashion it with our continuous cherishing. Cornelia Connelly spoke of a "love full of action." We choose to create an irresistible culture of tenderness that eliminates any creeping condescension that keeps us from being vulnerable with each other. As homie Gabriel puts it: "Here, we breathe kinship." Then we can imagine a fresh movement of resurrection communities where cherishing is what we do for a living. Kinship as a frequency.

The longest longitudinal study that ever came out of Harvard is the Harvard Study on Adult Development. They started with some 268 Harvard sophomores and followed them, their spouses, their children, and their grandchildren for eighty years. The study established the strong correlation between deep relationships and well-being. I suppose I would say "all relationships." Relational wholeness gets us to well-being. This is what the world is trying to be.

My great friend of nearly half a century, Paul Lipscomb, spent time with the Sandinistas in Nicaragua during the conflict between them and the Contras many years ago. He was with the Sandinistas one night in their encampment, and across the gulley, the Contras had made camp. He could hear the Contras arguing, drinking, carousing, and getting even drunker, while in the Sandinista camp they were singing and reciting poetry. The leader of the group turned to Paul and said, "That's why we will win, and they won't." A flourishing in love, endlessly created, in song and poetry. A contagion of tenderness under one roof, or a sky full of stars.

Freddy is blowing up my phone. It sits on the passenger seat as I'm driving from Seattle to Portland. It's insisting and jumping all over the seat like one of those Mexican jumping beans. I finally grab it. "THEY KILLED MORENO." Freddy is screaming and rocking the dead body of his great friend, Moreno, in his arms in the middle of the street. It was three in the afternoon. Freddy and Moreno were playing with neighborhood kids, a pickup game of football in the middle of Mott Street. A car of armed gang members drove by, saw Moreno, and ended his life. Freddy's sobbing is so wet and fulsome, it's hard to make out what he's saying.

Suddenly, a new voice arrives. "PUT THE PHONE DOWN." It's the police.

"But I'm talkin' to G. They killed Moreno." He's wailing his words.

"PUT THE FUCKING PHONE DOWN." The phone went dead.

I suspect it's part of police training to take control of all situations. To assume authority over it. And yet their way of proceeding elevated and exacerbated everything. Gasoline to flames. Everything suddenly got worse. Grieving Freddy was taken into custody. But it's not a huge stretch to imagine something different. To watch an officer crouch down next to Freddy as he rocked his dead friend. To rest his hand gently on Freddy's back until Freddy felt soothed enough to cooperate and let the police handle it from there. God's heartbeat. It looks like this when we see unshakable goodness and all-inclusive belonging. There would have been authority in this compassionate acceptance and total control in the momentary cherishing of a distraught gang member. Water on flames. Song and poetry. Safe. Seen. Cherished. Control of the situation wouldn't have been sacrificed but ensured.

I heard an LAPD detective explain how they investigate murders. "You have to imagine that the victim is a member of your family so as to give the investigation a sense of importance and urgency for you." God hopes that along with seeing the victim as a family member, we'll see the perpetrator as one, too. Wrapped in some unifying cloak.

There are a couple translations from a variety of Bibles of the word "repentance." Some render it as "change your mind." This seems to suggest that repentance is about shifting your opinion. I like the interpretation: "Move beyond the mind you have." It connotes an escape from a narrow mindset of views and opinions to a whole new way of seeing. From mere human thought to a mystical seeing. A redefining of "authority." Nothing short of that is what invites us.

Neuroscience tells us that we are wired to think the worst about ourselves and each other.

Cherishing rewires us to see the truth. Love believes the best about people. Love really does not allow us to do otherwise. Sergio says, "Love is large." There are no "good people" or "bad people," only God's people. Cherishing is what the world is trying to be. In the deepest part of ourselves, we all know that "two peas are better than one."

Luis is a self-admitted "shenanigizer," but, speaking to a room filled with every single judge in the state of Colorado at their annual judicial conference, he embodied his deepest dignity. He spoke of how he left prison, and he touted all the great programs in Los Angeles County. He received many certificates and was even placed in good jobs because of these programs. "And I STILL ended up sleeping on a park bench, drinking to get warm." Then "healing happened at Homeboy." We are always longing for an integrated wholeness. Love has the last word in that. Truly, the fastest route.

We belong with each other, and we need to cling to an insistence that no one is outside of that inclusion. After being locked up for eighteen years, Miguel now oversees security at our headquarters. He goes on a road trip with his wife to Oregon and they pass Crescent City, the northernmost tip of the state of California, and home to Pelican Bay, arguably one of the most notorious prisons in the country. He decides to drive inside the parking lot of the prison. The security guard screams at him about how this is trespassing and that folks aren't permitted here. Miguel rolls down his window and points at the prison: "I spent ten years, locked down, solitary confinement, in that place. I've been waiting for someone like you . . . to tell me I didn't belong here."

Heather McGhee in her fine book *The Sum of Us*, speaks of cross-racial public investment. In our country's underserved places, where disinvestment has been the rule, we invest in one another and this yields what she calls "solidarity dividends." Therein lies the sanctity of our interconnectedness: a functioning society that rests in a web of mutuality. We are always in search of a more powerful narrative of belonging.

On a weekly Zoom with homies during the pandemic, every Tuesday at 5:00 p.m., we'd reflect on some Scripture passage. Many in the group were homies who had been deported and are now living all over Mexico and Central America. One evening we discussed a passage about Jesus in the desert: "And angels ministered to him." Toward the end of our hour together, one homie said: "*La neta*, all of you on this Zoom—you are my angels—ministering to me."

There was a silence until Scrappy, from Mexicali, who normally has a pronounced stutter, stammers not a bit: "Wow. Thank you. No one ever called me an angel before." We are constantly investing in one another . . . our "solidarity dividend." We remind each other of our angel status. Living reminders that God revels in us. Ministering angels, cherishing with every breath, knowing that only from the heart can we touch the sky.

Indeed, "pilgrimage to the place of the wise is to find escape from the flame of separateness." A community of cherished belonging is the opposite of the illusion of separateness. Diabolical means "a separating." In weddings you hear, "What God has joined . . . don't separate." It's about something larger than divorce. To that end, we embrace, as fully as we can, our own suffering. The homies end up grateful for their struggle. They often say that they wouldn't have found their strength without it. It is an inner peace not dependent on how things turn out. This opens a door to be able to land on some spiritual intimacy with yourself and others.

As Adrian prepared to move on from Homeboy, he told me, "Compassion and kindness grew in me here." I suppose it is the delusional self-assertion about "what I bring" to this paltry table that gets transformed to be humble enough to receive from this sumptuous banquet. The place of the wise.

Stevie emphasizes, "Don't confuse insecurity with humility." Finally, it is our compassion that issues in a keen awareness of the interdependence of everything. "Open your hands," Rumi says, "if you want to be held."

One of our Jesuit volunteers, Lydia, drops us off at the airport for a flight to DC. As Marcos, Juan, and I get out of the car, Lydia hands us a small Tupperware full of brownies. It is a sweet and thoughtful thing to do. Once inside the airport, we are vexed by the Tupperware because we can't fit it into any of our bags. "Give me dat," Marcos says. Somehow, he was able to force it into the top of his open backpack but had difficulty fitting it there as well. Then he pulls around some jerry-rigged strap thing and, with great difficulty, clasps it. Then he looks at us and says, "Technology." We howl, and a catchphrase is born. Whenever we pull off the least impressive mechanical feat, like walking successfully through a rotating hotel door, someone would announce, "Technology."

Marcos, on the plane, after all the brownies had been dispatched, says, "Hey, what if we take a picture of us and this thing [the Tupperware . . . which he would later call "the Tumbleware"] in front of the White House, the Lincoln Memorial, and in front of that mountain with the presidents' faces carved into it." (I had to tell him that this last attraction is in South Dakota and that the DC Metro doesn't reach.) Faithfully, Marcos brings the "Tumbleware" wherever we go and sends the selfies back to Lydia. Oddly, we all feel held, with our hands open, by Marcos's mindfulness of someone who isn't with us. He finds real joy in allowing Lydia to be present and accounted for with kindness and a singular attention.

African American poet, Nikki Giovanni, in a *New York Times* interview at Christmastime, offered a reflection on the Little Drummer Boy. She says the kid "doesn't know how to read the room." He says, "I'm poor. All I have is this drum. May I play a song for you on my drum?" It is difficult for us to find real joy when our focus is what WE bring to the table. She suggests that the "little drummer girl" would have made herself useful, tidied up the stable, done something worthwhile. Like the mindfulness and singular attention of Marcos, being useful is "not about me." The girl rolls up her sleeves. In this way, she makes sure it stays about "us." Not about what we bring to the table, but the sumptuousness of the table. This is the wise place.

If God is love, then we are created in the image and likeness of love. David says that whenever he is stressed, he always plays this one song. It calms him down and he can find his center. It's "Oh My Love, Sweet Love" by the Hill Sisters. I was one year old when they recorded this song. I know lots of oldies. This wasn't one I knew. "I especially like the end," David says, when one of the women speaks while her sisters sing in the background. (They did this a lot in 1955.) In a sultry near whisper, she says, "I know you must be from above." David says it reminds him of his grandmother, who died not long ago, leaving him crestfallen. "My grandma was my protector." The love from above is anchored in the here and now. Yes, our image of God creates us. With the illusion of separateness gone, we find our center in love. We can then become each other's protector.

The vomiting begins before we even board the plane. I am taking Jeanette and Johanna to Chicago and Memphis. At LAX, Jeanette, the retching one, cannot be consoled. What I said about planes being safer than cars doesn't matter. "Oh yeah, well, cars don't go missing." You can't win. Without fail, Jeanette would go to every restaurant in these two cities and ask if things were good there. A premier seafood restaurant, "Is the seafood good here?" To THE best pizza place in Chicago . . . lines out the door. When finally it's our turn to order: "Is the deep-dish pizza good here?"

Johanna has a big "Fuck You" tattooed on her face. She is a beautiful woman who, at a painful, abusive juncture in her life, tried to put up a "Keep Away" sign. It would pain me to see waiters, strangers, even a mayor from a big city in Tennessee, recoil and audibly gasp when they turned and saw her. She seems inured to it. It rattles me every time. I just want to protect her from it.

When we have an afternoon break, she heads to the Brown Hotel to try their famous Hot Brown, an open-faced turkey sandwich with bacon and a Mornay sauce, invented a hundred years ago. She goes alone with that provocative face with the tattoo, which cannot be hidden by makeup, to try this local dish. Her venturing forth is an insistence on the sanctity of interconnectedness. Johanna is as brave as they get. Years later, she removes her tattoos, gets her degree in social work from UCLA, and is now a single mother attending UC Berkeley School of Law. As brave as they get.

Most of the day when I receive the Presidential Medal of Freedom from Joe Biden is now a surrealistic blur. A homie sends me a congratulatory text: "I heard you got a presidential pardon . . . or some shit like that." A homegirl, Ivy, stands in for me at a luncheon talk at which she says, "Father Greg couldn't be here today because he's at the White House, being knighted."

Each honoree is limited to eight guests. I have a niece, Klaya, who is a Secret Service agent, and she sneaks in as my ninth. Homies, staff, Jesuit Mark Torres, and my kid brother, Paul, and his wife, Joy, are there. The ceremony also honors Phil Donahue, and my brother walks up to Phil's wife, Marlo Thomas, who was the star of TV's *That Girl* in the '60s. "When I was a kid," Paul tells her, "I had a crush on you." She looks at him and deadpans, "Did you get over it?"

After the president secures the three snaps on the medal, he looks at me and whispers, "I'm reminded why they started the Jesuits. TO REFORM THE PAPACY." It was just random enough to leave us both laughing. EVERYONE afterward asked, "What did he say to you?"

They livestream the whole affair into Homeboy's expansive reception area, and folks at our headquarters stretch their necks around each other to see Joe Biden ad-lib about the Jesuits ("I love the Jebbies") and to hear the citation read by a straight-backed marine from the podium.

The meaning I gave to this entire event was certainly not lost on the hundreds clapping and weeping in that room at Homeboy. "It felt like he was putting that ribbon around our necks." "Damn, G . . . it was like all of us got that medal today." I'm glad they felt the honor of it, for people who have never been honored have a hard time honoring others. How honorable it is, then, to be loved into your own awakened heart. Of course, that's what heaven tastes like.

Ray Ray is a fixture at our place. He can't seem to find enough lift to raise himself out of chronic homelessness and repeated detentions. One morning, many years ago, he bumps into Father Mark in front of our old headquarters. He is, as the homies say, "tore up from the floor up." Ray Ray is dejected, dragging himself to even have this encounter with Mark. "They just let me out of jail and they took me in for nuh-thing." Ray Ray is now middle-aged, with a gang past and years of drug use and imprisonment behind him. He finds himself floating in a world that pays him no mind. He's unloading his woes. Mark is wearing this old leather jacket that he suddenly recalls is the one he used to wear on crisp, cool days when he ministered on the Blackfeet Indian Reservation. He reaches into an inner pocket and finds, still waiting there, a medicine pouch. Mark pulls it out and explains to Ray Ray, "The Blackfoot Native Americans, with whom I walked, gave me this medicine pouch when I left there." He reverently opens the bag, loosening its tie. He begins to retrieve the contents. "There is this arrowhead, which symbolizes courage. This tobacco stands for gratitude. This braided sweetgrass, blessing." Finally, Mark lifts out a meticulously folded ten-dollar bill. "This ten-dollar bill, they told me, is for emergencies and only emergencies." Mark holds it out in front of Ray Ray. "I think this counts as an emergency."

By the afternoon, Ray Ray returns jubilant. "That ten bucks did me a *paro* proper." He hands Mark a rolled-up wad of twenties, enfolded by a rubber band. He also comes to my office and hands me a similar-sized roll of bills. We never found out how the ten-dollar bill had been such a multiplier, but homies hitch their wagon often to the magical thinking of such things. He kept calling Mark's "medicine pouch" a "magical bag." Ray Ray returned a ten-dollar bill to Mark to replace the old one.

Some weeks later, the same scene unfolds. Ray Ray, at his wit's end, asking Mark for the ten spot from the "magical bag." Mark asks Ray Ray, "Is it an emergency? It has to be an emergency." Ray Ray assures him it is and Mark hands him the folded bill again. But days later it is "tore up from the floor up" Ray Ray again. The bill was spent. This time, no magical return on the ten-dollar investment. Mark quietly explains that "maybe it wasn't a real emergency." But maybe what is within our magical pouch is an ability to lift each other up "proper." When we choose to become emergency contact people in and out of emergencies.

I ask Tavo about his newborn son. "Is he talking yet?"

"Not really talking," Tavo clarifies, "but he's giving me hints." Tavo has been with us since his son was born. Tavo is undocumented. "I wasn't born here, but I came as soon as I could." He's come to a great understanding about his past gang life. He can even recalibrate the nuances of gang posturing. "I can see now that 'tough' is not the same as 'strong,'" he says. What made Jesus dangerous, in a sense, was his lack of fear. That was his strength. Jesus could touch the undying center in his soul and he simply wasn't afraid. Tavo as well. He found a community of cherished belonging, and it forged something that death couldn't touch. "You know, I gave up on my family a long-ass time ago. This is my family now. You know, this whole Homeboy thing . . . it really works." There is just one flesh we can wound. We find our oneness in that.

We all want to find our way out to the clearing, where we can see others beyond our tribes. Real kinship and connection takes time. "*Querer es poder*," the señoras at Dolores Mission Church would often say. "If you want to, you can do it." Intentionality is our superpower. It's the surest route, anyway. Part of our intentionality is to surrender and to cease fighting and stop resisting. Our surrender allows us to "open our hands" in order to "be held." What the world is trying to be is a wraparound place, where "belongance" is afforded to all. Breathe with your ears. Roshi Bernie Glassman said with some insistence: "Are we one or are we not?" Of course, another world is not only possible; every single one of us knows she's on her way. We can hear her breathing.

ACKNOWLEDGMENTS

YOU'RE ALWAYS GRATEFUL WHEN YOU KNOW WHAT YOU HAVE.
I am deeply appreciative to my agent, David McCormick, and editor, Jofie Ferrari-Adler. In them, I have two monuments of patience and gracious understanding. I am thankful for the whole team at Avid Reader Press and Simon & Schuster.

Eternally grateful to my Casa Luis Espinal Jesuit community and my provincial Sean Carroll. To Frank Buckley and Mark Torres for Purple Stole dinners and Homeboy accompaniment. To Paul DuRoss and the gang of the Bob Barry Invitational; to Laura Miera, Kate Bowler, Pete Holmes, and Rainn Wilson. To Mercedes Martinez and my exceptional board, Homeboy's executive team, and the beloved Council. I am so deeply appreciative of all our senior staff, core, and trainees at Homeboy. To Steve Delgado and Shirley Torres. To the beating hearts of Homeboy, Stevie, Hector, and José, and most especially to Tom Vozzo.

My heart is full of gratitude to Mary Rakow, Dave Mastrangelo, Maria Pollia, Jim Hayes, and Kevin O'Brien. Mario Prietto, Al Naucke, and John McGarry. Paul, Lynne, and Catherine Lipscomb for wisdom and tender friendship. To Nickie and all the Lipscombs. *Mil gracias* to Celeste, the Leaps, Matty and Katie, Ellie Hidalgo, John and Geri, Consuelo, Sandra Diana, Christina Dominguez, and Tom Bleich. Colin and Anna, Jim and Rob, Brian and Lynn, Buddy and Sara, Julie, Peg and Jim, Cara, Phil and Monica, Toto and Roberta. Thanks for the supreme guidance, Mirabai Starr and Jim Finley. To Ruben and Cristina. To the great John Lipson, MD, and North Star Bill Cain. To the wonderful Christy Juárez. To Sergio, my most wise spiritual director. To my sibs (see dedication). And to the thousands of homies and homegirls who have altered my heart forever. Indeed, I know what I have.

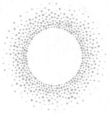

ABOUT THE AUTHOR

GREGORY BOYLE is an American Jesuit priest and the founder of Homeboy Industries in Los Angeles, the largest gang-intervention, rehabilitation, and reentry program in the world. In 2024, he was awarded the Presidential Medal of Freedom, the United States' highest civilian honor. He has received the California Peace Prize and been inducted into the California Hall of Fame. He received the University of Notre Dame's 2017 Laetare Medal, the oldest honor given to American Catholics. He is the acclaimed author of *Tattoos on the Heart*, *Barking to the Choir*, and *The Whole Language*. *Cherished Belonging* is his fourth book, and he will be donating all net proceeds to Homeboy Industries. Visit the author at HomeboyIndustries.org.

Avid Reader Press, an imprint of Simon & Schuster, is built on the idea that the most rewarding publishing has three common denominators: great books, published with intense focus, in true partnership. Thank you to the Avid Reader Press colleagues who collaborated on *Cherished Belonging*, as well as to the hundreds of professionals in the Simon & Schuster advertising, audio, communications, design, ebook, finance, human resources, legal, marketing, operations, production, sales, supply chain, subsidiary rights, and warehouse departments whose invaluable support and expertise benefit every one of our titles.

Editorial
Jofie Ferrari-Adler, *VP & Co-Publisher*
Carolyn Kelly, *Associate Editor*

Jacket Design
Alison Forner, *Senior Art Director*
Clay Smith, *Senior Designer*
Sydney Newman, *Art Associate*

Marketing
Meredith Vilarello, *Associate Publisher*
Katya Wiegmann, *Marketing and Publishing Assistant*

Production
Allison Green, *Managing Editor*
Rachael DeShano, *Senior Production Editor*
Alicia Brancato, *Production Manager*
Ruth Lee-Mui, *Interior Text Designer*
Cait Lamborne, *Ebook Developer*

Publicity
David Kass, *Senior Director of Publicity*
Rhina Garcia, *Publicist*
Eva Kerins, *Publicity Assistant*

Subsidiary Rights
Paul O'Halloran, *VP and Director of Subsidiary Rights*
Fiona Sharp, *Subsidiary Rights Coordinator*